Taste of Indonesia
Recipes from the Spice Islands

Tanah Lot Temple, Bali

Taste of Indonesia
Recipes from the Spice Islands

BY
Helena Soedjak, Ph.D.

Photographs
Harry Andree , M.D., Ph.D.

Introduction
John Bear, Ph.D.

SLG Books
Berkeley/Hong Kong

TASTE OF INDONESIA

SLG BOOKS
PO Box 9465 Berkeley, CA 94709
Tel: (510) 525-1134
Fax: (510) 525-2632
Email Indonesia@slgbooks.com
URL: www.slgbooks.com

Library of Congress Cataloging-in-Publication Data

Soedjak, Helena, 1957-
    Taste of Indonesia : recipes from the Spice Islands / by Helena Soedjak, ; photographs
  by Harry Andree.
      p. cm.
    Includes index.
    ISBN 0-943389-35-6 — ISBN 0-943389-34-8 (pbk.)
  1.   Cookery , Indonesian. I. Title.
    TX724.5.I5 S64 2001
    641.59593—DC21
                                                    2001020793

Printed in Hong Kong

Table of Contents

INTRODUCTION

How can something this big be nearly invisible?

Let's try this two-item quiz to help me make my point. Here are two questions; one demographic, and one culinary.

Demographic question:
Where, among the world's one hundred largest countries by population, does Indonesia rank? Or is it even in the top one hundred?

Answer: Would you believe it is #4. There it sits, bigger than Russia, bigger than Great Britain, bigger than France, bigger than Germany. And yet the typical American (and if that's you, don't feel bad; you have plenty of company) knows almost nothing about the land, the people, what language they speak, how they live, and (significantly) what they eat.

Thus we segué into question number two, the culinary one. In three words or more, state everything you know about the cuisine of this immense nation called Indonesia.

That "three words or more" was carefully worded, since extensive research has shown (I asked nine friends) that most people know only two words to describe Indonesian cuisine: (1) rice and (2) table. Rice table. Or, in Dutch, one word: rijsttafel.

What a shame! It is as if the only word that Europeans or Asians had to describe food in America was "Picnic" or "McDonalds."

If Americans have had any taste of Indonesian food, it probably came on a rare visit to something called a "rice table" at the only Indonesian restaurant within fifty miles.

In San Francisco, that gourmet center of the western world, the phone book lists over 300 Chinese restaurants, hundreds of Japanese, Italian, Mexican and Thai restaurants. But Indonesian: you can count them on the fingers of one hand, and still have enough fingers left over to type or to scratch your head to wonder what's wrong with us?

How can a nation that loves its food, and has a Thai restaurant in even the smallest towns, a pizza place in every neighborhood, and a Chinese restaurant every three blocks, fail to have embraced Indonesian cooking, both in the restaurant and, most importantly and relevantly, in the home.

Fess up. When was the last time you made chicken livers with shrimp and coconut, duck with lime sauce, or the dessert (yes, dessert) called rice filled with chicken?

You see, most of us just aren't attuned to thinking about Indonesian cuisine. When the question arises, "What shall I make for dinner when the Finchleys come to dinner next week," you didn't even consider for a moment the possibility of stir-fried shrimp with ginger, steamed ginger chicken, stewed beef in red coconut sauce, or other Indonesian treats. I can assure you that old Mrs. Finchley would have loved any of these, and probably changed her will in your favor as soon as she got home.

The beauty (figuratively) of *Taste of Indonesia* is that Helena Soedjak solves all of our Indonesia-related deficiencies in one fell swoop. She tells us about the history. The culture. And the food. Indeed, she tells us a great deal about her native land and its peoples, from the great temple of Borobudur to the native craft called Batik. And she not only communicates her love of Indonesian cuisine, but she shows us how to prepare and serve a great many (93, to be exact) dishes, from soup (vegetable coconut soup, for instance) to nuts (how about gado-gado salad with peanut dressing).

And none of the recipes is called "rice table" (although they may be served with or on rice, and may be eaten on a table).

The beauty (literally) of this book is in the magnificent photographs available on the accompanying CD, some of the finest food photography you'll ever see. Indeed, if there were a Pulitzer Prize category for best photography by a person with two doctorates who teaches in a major medical school, Harry Andree would be a sure thing.

Author and superb chef Helena Soedjak has only one doctorate: it is in biochemistry from the University of California, but she holds patents for her inventions in food technology.

It is clear, however, from *Taste of Indonesia*, that many of her finest inventions (and discoveries) have not passed through the patent office in Washington. Lamb turnovers. Avocado fruit cocktail. Cat tongue cookies. Filled Chinese eggplant. Sweet and spicy fruit salad. Vegetable soup over filled omelet. I don't need to repeat the entire table of contents for you here, but I wanted to be sure to mention some of my favorites.

The semifinal thing to say about this splendid book is that it makes Indonesian cooking absolutely accessible to anyone. The ingredients can be easily found, and the cooking style does not require a Ph.D., even if the author, the photographer, and even the introduction-writer happen to have one. (An "all doctor" cast. Heck, the guy who ran the printing press probably teaches neurosurgery on the side.)

The final thing to say, and then you can get on with buying the book, or starting to steam the spuds for your Crispy Filled Potato, if you already own the book, is that what you have here is SLG Books' first entry into the world of multi-media publishing. Not only is the text of the book as diverse and eclectic as one might ever find, covering history, art, music, religion, travel, and fabrics of Indonesia, in addition to cuisine, but the CD adds an important new dimension.

Sorry there aren't 'scratch and sniff' panels so you can start salivating over Indonesian barbecue ribs before you actually cook them. And we haven't yet perfected the toll-free phone service where you can listen to the publisher banging out Javanese hit songs on his gamelan. Perhaps by the third printing; stand by.

No, come to think of it, don't stand by. Ambulate into your kitchen, and begin the modest but immensely fulfilling labors that will result in you and your family, friends, or dinner guests experiencing the absolutely splendid taste of Indonesia.

John Bear
Berkeley, California

PREFACE

Indonesian cuisine has not received the attention it deserves, partly because of the obscurity of its exotic ingredients and method of preparation. Many believe the dishes are too complicated and time consuming to prepare. In this book I will demonstrate that delectable Indonesian foods can be made simply and conveniently. They can have an exotic flavor and be appetizingly served, but at the same time are easy to prepare.

The cooking techniques and tips described in this book are designed to maintain the dishes' authenticity while adapting them to our contemporary lifestyle. All ingredients are measured using standard American measuring equipment so that the recipes are reproducible even by novice cooks. About half of the recipes will take less than 30 minutes to cook. Others will take a little longer, but will still require minimal preparation time. All of the ingredients are readily available, either in regular supermarkets or Oriental grocery stores.

Many of the dishes can be refrigerated for a few days or frozen for a long time. This is convenient because large quantities of a dish can be prepared and frozen until needed. In some cases, advance preparation will enhance the taste since it allows intense penetration of the spices into the food. The exceptions are stir-fried vegetables and deep-fried seafood, which are better when served fresh and crispy.

The dishes in this cookbook represent popular foods on Java Island, or more specifically East Java, where I grew up. Although some dishes are similar, food varies considerably from one Indonesian island to another. The islands are isolated from each other by great distances and endowed with different natural resources. The diverse religions are also an important factor for the culinary traditions on the islands since the religions govern the type of meat to be used for cooking. Today Islam (in Sumatra, Java, Lombok, and Sumbawa), Hinduism (in Bali and Java), Christianity (in Flores, Timor, Ambon, and some parts of Celebes and Moluccas), and Buddhism (in Java) are practiced throughout the country. The complex fusion of Buddhist, Hindu and Islamic influences in Java results in a special blend of cuisine and culture. The Indonesian cuisine is a symphony of color, texture and flavor, with plenty of variety and sophistication.

Rice is the basis of every meal in most places, except in some remote inland areas, or in the Moluccas, where sago (palm pith) and cassava root (tapioca) represent the most important food staple. In Bali other starches (cassava root, sweet potatoes and corn) occasionally replace rice. Many households serve rice three times a day. Breakfast is usually simple and light. More elaborate meals are served for lunch and dinner.

Soup is not served at the beginning of a meal as in a Western meal. Instead it is brought to the table together with all other dishes. The typical menu consists of cooked white rice served with as many as five dishes, made up of fish, vegetables, eggs, poultry or beef. All dishes are placed in the middle of the table and everyone helps himself to the food. The dishes should complement each other in taste, texture and color. Chili sauce (*sambal*) is always served as a condiment. The fish is usually fried, roasted over charcoal or simmered in coconut milk. Indonesians are also fond of salted and dried fish. Vegetables are served raw with chili sauce or cooked. Chicken is the most popular poultry. Meat is usually beef because the majority of the population is Moslem. In fact, beef is so popular that in the Indonesian language, meat means beef, unless some other kind of meat is specified. In Bali, where the majority of the population is Hindu, pork is preferred, because cows are considered sacred. Lamb is not common in Indonesia since sheep do not tolerate the tropical climate. Instead goat meat is consumed.

Water, tea, or exotic native fresh fruit juices are commonly served with ice at most meals. Tea with a strong flowery flavor, such as jasmine tea, is usually preferred; it may be sweetened. Alcoholic beverages are not commonly drunk at mealtime, although many Westerners think that beer or a fruity white wine, especially a Gewürztraminer, goes well with Indonesian food. Although grape wine is not popular among Indonesians, there exist several types of alcoholic beverages made from native plants, such as *tuak* made from fermented sap of the inflorescence of coconut palm and *arak ketan* made from fermented white or red glutinous rice.

Indonesian desserts do not include cakes or anything else that is rich. Instead light desserts, such as fresh fruit or fruit drinks, are preferred. Sometimes sorbet or ice cream is served. Although sweets and cakes are popular, they are eaten as snacks at anytime in-between meals.

My education in cookery began when as a young girl I watched our cook or my mother preparing foods in the kitchen (In Indonesia household cooks are quite common). I picked up most of the cooking techniques, which form my basic knowledge today, by observing and sometimes helping in the kitchen.

Like most kitchens in Indonesia, ours was located in a separate wing away from the main portion of the house. The kitchen was well ventilated since the one side of this room was completely open to the backyard, except for the low back wall protecting the four side-by-side gas-flamed burners. A wood-fired stove and a charcoal grill were placed outside. The oven, which was used more for baking cakes than cooking foods, was kept in a separate room. (Indonesian cooks prefer to use a grill rather than an oven for most cooking).

Our cook was always busy in the kitchen. The fragrant smell of fresh lemongrass, galangal, simmering spices in coconut milk, and grilled meat often filled the room. When I was bored with playing or doing homework, I often went to the kitchen. There was always something to see and eat there (I called it tasting).

We grew most of the spices in our backyard and picked them fresh as needed. We even had several banana and papaya trees, which were grown not only for their fruit but also for their leaves. Indonesians use banana leaves for wrapping food to be grilled or steamed. The leaves impart a subtle yet wonderful flavor to the food. Papaya leaves are used to wrap meat, especially during marination. The natural enzyme (papain) in the papaya leaves tenderizes the meat.

Our cook often took me to the market on Sundays at six o'clock in the morning. At seven o'clock the market was already crowded and noisy as merchants and customers talked and bargained loudly. The market offered everything from spices, arrays of tropical fruits and raw ingredients (meat, fish, seafood and produce) to a great selection of ready-to-eat snacks. The potpourri of color and aroma was overwhelming. As she meticulously chose her ingredients, she taught me how to select meat, fish, eggs or vegetables. In the last few years many supermarkets have been built in the cities. Although the traditional markets still exist today, most people in the cities get their groceries from supermarkets.

I left Indonesia after high school and went to Germany to study. Although I enjoyed eating lunch at the school cafeteria, I was reluctant to eat dinner there because only cold foods such as salad and sandwiches were served. For dinner I preferred warm foods, so I decided to prepare my own dinner. I discovered that Indonesian cooking was not as difficult and complicated as I had believed.

While in Germany, I had limited access to ingredients used in traditional Indonesian dishes. Fortunately I was able to buy many ingredients from some Indonesian students who regularly traveled to Holland where there are many Indonesian stores. Many Indonesians immigrated to Holland after Indonesia claimed its independence in 1945. Some of these immigrants opened Indonesian restaurants and *toko* (stores) selling cooked foods and ingredients. After I received my degree in Germany, I moved to Holland and lived there for nearly two years before I moved to the United States.

While living abroad I learned to modify and simplify the traditional Indonesian cooking without sacrificing its genuine taste. For example, instead of using fresh spices, I substituted dried ground spices for daily cooking. Although fresh spices are more flavorful, their powdered form is easier to store and ready-to-use, thus reducing the time and preparation significantly.

All good cooks are formed through experience, creativity, and keeping an open mind. Cooking is more than following rules. It is also interpreting recipes and knowing how to adapt them to fit your taste. My interest in cooking came from my mother. Every time I praised the food served at home, at parties or in restaurants, my mother took the time to explain how it was prepared. Sometimes she would even add a few useful tips of her own. Her instructions and tips built my understanding of the basics required for cooking Indonesian dishes. Thus I learned how to prepare food from its taste and appearance. Occasionally I still ask her advice on a recipe.

This book is intended to provide basic instructions to those who desire a taste of good Indonesian food without having to spend an entire day in the kitchen. It is also a tribute to my mother.

ABOUT INDONESIA

GEOGRAPHY, HISTORY AND CULTURE

Indonesia is located in Southeast Asia astride the equator. It consists of more than 17,000 islands, of which less than 3,000 are inhabited. These islands are scattered throughout a 3,200-mile (5,100 kilometers) stretch of ocean forming the world's largest archipelago with a span as wide as the area between California and Bermuda.

The largest islands are *Kalimantan* (Borneo), *Sumatra, Jawa* (Java), *Sulawesi* (Celebes) and *Irian Jaya* (West New Guinea). Territories on these five islands make up 90% of Indonesia. The archipelago is believed to be one of the earliest places that human beings ever lived.

There are only two seasons: rainy and dry. The length of the days and nights is more or less equal all year long. Near sea level it is hot and humid with temperatures ranging from 74 - 88° F (23 - 31° C), but up in the hills and mountains it is cooler. The soil nutrients are replenished by frequent volcanic eruptions. The ashes from eruptions are a short-term calamity, but in the long run bless the area with fertility. The famous Krakatau eruption in 1883 destroyed a large portion of the island and killed 36,000 people. More than half of the country's land area is covered by jungles, which account for 10% of the world's tropical forests. These forests are home to 4,000 varieties of trees, 30,000 species of flowering plants (including 5,000 species of orchids), 500 species of mammals and more than 1,500 different kinds of birds. Many of these unique flora and fauna cannot be found elsewhere in the world. The world's largest flower, *Rafflesia*, with a diameter of 3 ft. and a weight of 20 lbs., is unique to Indonesia.

Due to its strategic location and wealth in natural resources and crops, sailors and traders came to Indonesia as early as the first century to trade and settle. The early settlers (Indian, Chinese and Arab) influenced the religion, language, literature, music, art and cuisine. Indian spice merchants arrived in Sumatra and Java as early as the 2nd century. Then Arab spice traders arrived about 1400 A.D. to look for spices. Many of them remained and replaced the existing religions of Hinduism and Buddhism with Islam.

Today Islam is the dominant religion in Indonesia and is practiced by nearly 88% of the population, whereas Hinduism and Buddhism account for only 2%. Christianity (Protestant and Roman Catholic) represents 10% of the society.

European sailors and traders came later on for the spice trade. At that time spices were more expensive than gold or jewels. Marco Polo was the first European explorer to visit Sumatra and the neighboring islands in the thirteenth century. He called the Moluccas the Spice Islands due to their abundance in pepper, cloves, cinnamon and nutmeg. Then came the Portuguese in the sixteenth century, followed by the Dutch, who in 1602 formed the Dutch East India Company to monopolize the entire spice trading.

By 1668 the Dutch extended their authority over most of the islands and exploited the natural resources of the islands: spices, agricultural produce and minerals. In 1942 the Japanese occupied the archipelago. Following Japan's surrender to the Allies at the end of World War II in August 1945 Indonesia declared its independence. Although the Dutch attempted to reassert control over the islands, they finally agreed to transfer sovereignty to Indonesia in August 1949.

The economic subsistence of Indonesia has changed dramatically since its independence. In 1962 Indonesia became a member of OPEC (Organization of Petroleum Exporting Countries). Today petroleum, natural gas and minerals account for the highest export earnings, although agriculture continues to be the mainstay of the economy. Forestry products represent the country's second-largest export. Indonesia is the world's largest producer of liquefied natural gas and the world's third largest tin producer after Malaysia and Thailand. Bauxite, nickel, coal, iron core and copper are also abundant on the islands.

Indonesia is ranked as the world's fourth most populous nation after China, India and the United States. More than 190 million people from over 300 distinct ethnic groups inhabit the archipelago, making it one of the most ethnically diverse populations in the world. The largest ethnic group is the Javanese, who constitute 40-50% of the population. The largest non-indigenous group is the Chinese, who live mainly in the urban areas and constitute about 3% of the total population. More than 200 distinct languages are spoken locally, but the official language is *Bahasa Indonesia.* This national language along with the common way of life unifies the vast variety of ethnic groups, as reflected by the national motto *"Bhinneka Tunggal Ika,"* meaning "Unity in Diversity."

The bond among families or friends is strong. Indonesians enjoy getting together. Foods or snacks are usually served in meetings or gatherings. It is also common to invite unexpected guests to stay for meals as a gesture of hospitality and welcome. Communal, religious and family feasts are important occasions in daily life. An important communal feast for the Javanese called *selamatan* is a celebration for illness recovery, new house, marriage, childbirth and any other

important occasion. *Selamatan* may also be held to commemorate a death, dispel bad luck or invite good fortune. The foods can be simple or festive and are shared with relatives, friends and neighbors. They may be invited to come over or the food may be delivered to their house. The food used for *selamatan* is traditionally comprised of a plate of cone-shaped rice as the centerpiece that is decorated lavishly with many variety of side dishes. The recipes for many of the dishes can be found in this cookbook. This beautifully prepared food, called *nasi tumpeng* (*nasi* means cooked rice), is a work of art that impressed the Dutch during their colonial time in Indonesia. They adapted the idea of serving rice with a variety of Indonesian savory side dishes to their life style and called it *rijsttafel*, a Dutch word which literally means, "rice table." Today the word *rijsttafel* in Holland often refers to an elaborate Indonesian menu.

ARTS AND MUSIC

Indonesia has a rich ancient cultural history. Magnificent Hindu and Buddhist temples existed centuries before Europe's great Gothic cathedrals were built. Indonesian fine arts—batik (wax-resist dyeing method), *wayang kulit* (shadow puppet), *gamelan* music and traditional dances—have been part of Indonesians' social and cultural life for centuries. Artistically cultivated rice terraces (*sawah*) have been developed in Java and Bali since ancient time, applying an elaborate and ingenious irrigation system to channel water from lakes, rivers and springs.

Borobudur: the magnificent Buddhist temple

Borobudur, which was built in central Java about 800 A.D. under the Sailendra dynasty, is one of the world's greatest and most impressive monuments. It is a Buddhist temple that contains a complete exposition of doctrine. The whole monument is made of stone pieces that were assembled with great precision.

The entire structure is set on a large square plinth (403 ft. on each side) and consists of five square terraces gradually diminishing in size. There are stairways in the center of each side of the terrace providing access to the upper terrace. As you climb through the stairways, you will see relief sculptures that symbolize a Buddhist transition from the lowest manifestations toward nirvana (spiritual freedom). The reliefs at the lowest level illustrate the causal effect of good and bad deeds in everyday life through successive reincarnations. The second level illustrates the historical life of Buddha, and the upper levels contain themes that are more profound and metaphysical.

Above the fifth terrace stand three open gradated circular terraces, which carry 72 bell-shaped perforated Buddhist shrines (*stupas*). Each *stupa* contains a huge stone meditative Buddha half-visible through the perforated stonework, symbolizing incomplete states of enlightenment. In the center of the top terrace sits the main *stupa*—the largest *stupa* in the monument—that contains an unfinished image of Buddha, symbolizing the indefinable ultimate spiritual state.

The monument was neglected from about 1000 A.D. and overgrown with vegetation until restored by Dutch archaeologists between 1907 and 1911. The Indonesian government began a massive restoration project in 1975 to preserve the national treasure.

Batik : the original Javanese craft

Batik is a wax-resist dyeing process originally used by the Javanese. The technique involves applying molten wax to cover patterned areas so they will not receive the color. Traditionally cotton is the fabric of choice, but now silk is also used. First the design is drawn onto the cloth, then the wax is applied, typically with a bamboo stick or spouted applicator. After the fabric has been dyed the wax is removed by scraping or boiling the fabric. Multicolored and blended effects are obtained by repeating the dyeing process several times, with the initial wax boiled off and a new wax pattern applied before re-dyeing. Classical designs include traditional abstract motifs. For decorative items, landscape and shadow puppet motifs are popular. A new wax-application technique using paintbrushes has been developed recently to produce a freestyle design. Batik is used for clothes, linens, tablecloths, scarves and decorative items. Now the official national attire is also made of batik.

Shadow puppet (*wayang kulit*): the ancient theater

Shadow puppet plays involves a single seated puppeteer (*dalang*) who manipulates the puppets, sings, chants narration, conducts the orchestra and articulates the dialogue. The puppet figures are made of leather that is carved (according to fixed patterns for nose, eyes, gaze, stance, body build and costume) to indicate the character type and status. For example, demons are characterized by a large nose and protruding eyes, while civilized figures have almond-shaped eyes looking downward. The figures are intricately incised to allow light to pass through them and are attached to sticks for more fluid manipulation. The puppeteer sits behind the screen and is invisible to the audience. A lamp creates a lacy shadow as the puppet is pressed against the back of a vertical screen of white cloth. The puppeteer moves the puppets away from and towards the screen to create an impression of movement and distance. This effect can be enhanced by a brisk swing of the lamp.

The performance is accompanied by the music played by the *gamelan* ensemble (described below). The music captures the character, mood and action of the scene. The plays are set in mythological times, some relating to indigenous animistic festivals and worship of local spirits or dramatizing episodes from the traditional *Ramayana* and *Mahabarata* Hindu epics, but the majority are essentially Javanese creations depicting five heroic Pandawa brothers. Each play consists of three parts and lasts up to ten hours.

Gamelan : the sound of moonlight

The *gamelan* is an orchestra dominated by bronze percussion instruments. It derives its name from *gamel*, an old Javanese word for handle or hammer. The haunting and hypnotic sound of the *gamelan* may best be described as a symphony of moonlight and rippling water.

The instruments in the ensemble consist of several varieties of gongs and metallophones (xylophone-like instruments with metal keys that are struck with mallets). The gongs are either placed horizontally (the *bonang*) or vertically. The metallophones have bronze keys lying over wooden trough resonators (the *saron*) or on bamboo resonators (the *gender*). Other contributing instruments are the wooden drum with skins stretched over both ends (the *kendang*), wooden xylophone (the *gambang*), zither with metal strings (the *celempung*), bamboo flute (the *suling*), and the two-stringed bowed lute (the *rebab*).

Gamelan music has played a focal role in the Javanese and Balinese cultures for centuries. It is used to accompany the entire range of performing arts (dance, drama, puppet shows, sung poetry or theater), but is also enjoyed on its own.

Rice terraces (*sawah*): rice farming using ingenious irrigation system

Rice is the cornerstone of the meal for most Indonesians and is treated with much respect. Its production is more efficient in wetlands. Therefore riverbeds are a favorable site for rice cultivation. In Southeast Asia large areas of the terrain consist of mountains and hills. As early as the 11th century, in order to make this land available for producing food the Javanese and Balinese developed an intricate system of irrigation, by building terraces. The rice terraces not only prevent erosion of the otherwise meager fertile soil by reducing the water flow, but also give every farmer enough water to cultivate his rice. The terraces have been essential to feed the densely populated island of Java. Shaped like a stairway to the sky, the terraces create the beautiful and characteristic landscape of Java and Bali.

The irrigation system strongly affects the Indonesians' way of life. Maintenance of the terraces is labor intensive and requires cooperation among the farmers. Tasks are usually divided. Men plow the fields using water buffaloes (*kerbau*). They construct as well as maintain the canals for the distribution of water. Women plant the rice seedlings by hand, protect the seedlings from weeds and harvest the mature rice. Children participate by caring for the water buffaloes and protecting the maturing rice from birds.

The harvest takes place two or three times a year. During harvest times ceremonies are performed to honor the Goddess Dewi Sri who is believed to take care of the rice fields. For these celebrations the village women work together to prepare elaborate dishes. Shadow puppet plays and *gamelan* orchestras enhance the harvest feast.

FAMOUS FOOD SPECIALTIES

Sate : the sizzling grilled meat on skewers

What could be more Indonesian than *sate*? It is said that *sate* originated in Java centuries ago. *Sate* is marinated bite-sized meat cubes threaded on bamboo sticks and quickly broiled on glowing, not flaming, charcoal. There are many different varieties of *sate*, depending on the type of meat, marinade or dipping sauce used. Chicken is mostly used, although beef, pork, goat and seafood are also common. The prevalent dipping sauces are sweet soy sauce and peanut sauce.

The meat is continuously basted with marinade and the skewers are turned every 3 to 5 minutes until the meat is brown on both sides. Since the meat is rather small, they get cooked quickly. The meat is dipped in the sauce and eaten right off the skewer.

Sate is served not only at mealtime, but also as a snack between meals or after supper. Today in Java you see *sate* vendors shuffling through the streets after sunset with their handcrafted tripods *(pikulan)* on their shoulders. Fully equipped with the ingredients and grill apparatus, the vendor is ready to cook the food in front of his customer. Since the meat and the charcoal are already prepared in advance, the vendor needs only to grill the meat over the charcoal fire and the *sate* is ready in a few minutes. Most Indonesian customers are loyal to their favorite vendor. Sometimes the customers call on the vendors to cater large quantities of their specialties to parties and gatherings.

If a charcoal grill is unavailable, it is possible to broil *sate* in a gas or electric oven. This method, however, will not deliver the same aroma and taste that meets Indonesians' standard for *sate*.

Chilies and chili sauce (*sambal*): the appetite trigger

There are two varieties of chilies in Indonesia: small and large. Small chilies (*cabai rawit*) are served on the table as a condiment in whole or sliced pieces and sometimes mixed with soy sauce. Large red chilies are used in sauces, whereas large green chilies are cooked as vegetables. Chilies are also served in the form of a ground paste called *sambal* as a condiment or seasoning.

The small chilies are the hottest. Most of the hotness comes from the seeds and ribs, which can be removed for a milder flavor. The seeds and ribs contain oil that can cause irritation, rash or even a burn. Wash cut chilies under cold running water: hot water can release irritating vapors. It is important to wash your hands afterwards with soap and warm water before touching your face or eyes.

In the United States Indonesian chilies are available only in Asian markets. However, the Mexican jalapeno peppers, which are more readily available in regular supermarkets, are an acceptable substitute. While most Indonesian recipes call for fresh chilies, occasionally dried chilies can be substituted. To use dried chilies, soak them in hot water for 10 minutes to make them soft. The recipes in this book use ready-made *sambals* as a substitute for ground large red chilies.

In Indonesia no meal is considered complete without a *sambal*. There are a great variety of *sambals*, but each one is unique for its distinct flavor and is used to complement a specific dish. In Indonesia *sambals* are always made fresh shortly before being served. In the United States ready-made *sambals*, made from large red chilies and stored in plastic or glass jars, are available in Asian markets. This *sambal* will keep for a long time in the refrigerator.

Indonesia's hot and humid climate suppresses one's appetite. It is said that *sambal* stimulates the appetite. *Sambal* is used sparingly as a condiment. If you use too much, the best way to alleviate the burning sensation on the tongue is to eat more rice or a slice of raw cucumber. Drinking will only palliate the heat temporarily. This may, in fact, be how the sambal increases the appetite.

Gado-gado: the zesty peanut dressing salad

A traditional Indonesian *gado-gado* dish uses specialty vegetables—such as *tempe* (fermented soybean cake), bean curd, bean sprouts, yard-long beans and *kangkung* (a kind of water spinach). *Tempe* and bean curd are deep-fried, then cut into bite-size pieces. Bean sprouts are steamed or blanched. Yard-long beans and *kangkung* are cut into two-inch pieces, then steamed or blanched. *Tempe*, yard-long beans and *kangkung* are available in Asian markets. These vegetables can be replaced by other fresh vegetables without jeopardizing the authenticity of the recipe. After all, it is always the dressing that gives the name and identity to salads. Substituting cooked vegetables with fresh ones offers simplicity and perhaps also enticement to the Western taste.

Krupuk: the magic crackers

Krupuk is the famous Indonesian cracker. It is rich in taste and crunchy in texture. A big jar of fried *krupuk* can almost always be found in every household. It is often served at mealtime, but is also eaten as a snack. There are different varieties (by flavor, size, or shape) of *krupuk*; for example *krupuk udang* is made from shrimp and *krupuk ikan* is made from fish. Regardless of the variety, the basic ingredients are flour, egg, salt, flavoring and sometimes coloring. The proportions of shrimp or fish to the flour determine the quality and price. A good quality *krupuk udang* contains mainly shrimp and only a small amount of flour. Less expensive restaurants and street vendors usually offer *krupuk* made from flour only.

To make *krupuk*, a dough with the chosen ingredients is prepared. Then the dough is shaped into loaves, steamed and sliced. The slices are allowed to dry in the sun. Once dried, the *krupuk* should be stored in an airtight container. If it absorbs moisture and becomes damp, it should be dried again in the sun or in an oven (at low heat for 10 minutes) prior to frying. Ready-to-fry *krupuk* is available in Asian markets. When deep-fried in oil, the *krupuk* puffs up to double or triple its original size. For the best taste, fried *krupuk* should not be kept too long, unless it is stored in an airtight container.

FOOD PREPARATION AND UTENSILS

Rice: the centerpiece of the feast

A wide variety of rice is available in Indonesia, but long-grain polished white rice is the most popular. The fragrant Thai varieties available in the West are probably the closest in taste to good Indonesian rice. Although many varieties of cooked rice—*nasi gurih* (rich coconut rice), *nasi kuning* (yellow savoury rice), *nasi uduk* (fragrant spiced coconut rice), *nasi tumpeng* (festive rice), *nasi langi* (yellow rice), and *nasi ulam* (spiced rice)— are popular, *nasi putih (*plain cooked white rice) is served for daily consumption. Glutinous rice *(ketan)*, sometimes also called sticky rice or sweet rice, is used only for sweet snacks or desserts. This rice becomes sticky when cooked.

Indonesians have many ways of cooking rice. The old traditional way is to steam it in a pan with a pleated bamboo colander, cooked over a wood fire, which gives the rice a special taste. Today most households in the cities cook rice using a stove or an electric rice cooker. In the United States Rice cookers are available in most department stores and Asian shops.

Stove-top

Place rice in a pot. Select the size of the pot so that the rice does not fill more than two thirds of the pot, because the rice will expand when cooked. Add water to the rice so that the water level reaches about 3/4 inch above the rice. Indonesian cooks commonly measure the water level to the first joint of their forefingers. Cook the rice uncovered over moderate heat. If foaming occurs, lower the heat slightly so that the contents of the pot do not foam over the rim. When the liquid almost completely boils away, cover the pot. Continue to cook for an additional 10 minutes over the lowest possible heat. (If the heat is too high, a crust of rice will form at the bottom of the pot.) Then remove the pot from the stove and let it sit covered for at least 5 minutes. This way the rice will not stick to the bottom.

Microwave

Rice can also be cooked in a microwave following the same procedure for stovetop preparation. The only difference is the source of heat. The rice is cooked in an uncovered container until the liquid is almost completely absorbed. Then the container is covered with a lid and cooking is continued for an additional 4-10 minutes, depending on the amount of rice or the power of the microwave.

Rice cooker

Place rice in a pot with the same amount of water described for stovetop cooking, then turn the switch on. When the rice is done, the cooker will switch off automatically. Let the rice sit in the cooker for a few minutes. This way the rice will not stick to the bottom of the cooker.

Tips

Cooked rice retains its heat for a long time. This allows the rice to be prepared in advance. The rule of thumb is that a cup of uncooked rice will serve three people. However, it is better to cook more than expected, since any leftover may be reused. Leftover rice can be stored in a covered container in the refrigerator for a few days. Cold cooked rice may be warmed by steaming or microwaving. To microwave, first sprinkle rice with water, then cover with a lid or plastic sheet. The rice becomes rather hard and dry upon refrigeration. The addition of water softens and moistens the rice. Leftover steamed rice is good for fried rice; freshly cooked rice is too wet for fried rice. When preparing fried rice, it is not necessary to reheat the rice.

Deep-frying: the light, crisp way

Deep-frying is one of the most popular cooking techniques throughout Southeast Asia. This cooking technique may have evolved in ancient times as a means to preserve foods since microorganisms can propagate rapidly in tropical climates. The heat sterilizes and slightly dehydrates the food, thereby increasing the shelf life. Deep-fried foods are often perceived as greasy. However, when prepared properly, deep-fried foods can be light, crispy and nutritious.

In the past Indonesians preferred coconut oil for cooking and deep frying, because the oil imparts a wonderful flavor to the food. However, palm oil, palm kernel oil and corn oil are more widely used nowadays.

For the best results, the food must be completely immersed in the oil, which should be at least 2 inches deep. The wok serves as the best utensil for deep-frying since its round-bottom form enables us to use less oil. Generally, 1-2_ cups of oil are required.

Cooking at the right temperature is the key to success in deep-frying. It should be between 360-380° F. At this temperature, the surface of the food is sealed, preventing absorption of the oil. It is important to wait until the oil reaches this temperature before frying or the food will become soft and greasy. The oil should not be heated beyond 400° F, which is food will become soft and greasy. The oil should not be heated beyond 400° F, which is evident when the oil begins to smoke. If the oil is too hot, the outside of the food will burn before it is fully cooked inside. Moreover, overheating impairs the quality of the oil, resulting in darkening and a poor flavor. To test the oil temperature, drop a small piece of garlic or onion into the oil. If it rises quickly and begins to turn light brown without burning, the oil is at the right temperature. If it remains at the bottom, the oil is not hot enough.

The oil can be reused, but not too often. Discard the oil when it smells, changes color or after frying fish. The oil retains the fish flavor and will affect the taste of any other deep-fried food. Keep the used oil in a sealed jar in a cool dark place. Remove any breading or food particles before storing the oil to preserve the quality. The particles can be removed by straining the oil through a mesh skimmer, cheesecloth or a fine-weave strainer. An easier way to remove the residue is by pouring the oil into a jar. After the particles have settled pour the oil carefully into another jar leaving the residue at the bottom of the first jar.

After removing the fried food from the hot oil it should be drained on a plate lined with a double layer of absorbent paper. Allow the food to rest on the plate for a few minutes and you will see that most of the oil is absorbed by the paper.

Fried shallots and garlic: the magic garnish and flavoring

Fried shallots and garlic are used in many Indonesian dishes, especially in soups and stews. Fried shallots are not only added while cooking, but sometimes sprinkled to the food shortly before serving for garnishing and adding extra flavor. I call it a finishing touch. I often prepare a lot of fried shallots and garlic in my spare time and have them available when I need them. This saves much time later on and makes cooking more enjoyable.

In Indonesia, shallots *(bawang merah)* are used almost exclusively in cooking. Large onions *(bawang Bombay)* are used as a vegetable in stir-fried dishes. Although shallots are more suitable for Indonesian cooking, onions may be used.

First peel shallots, then slice them thinly and evenly crosswise. When large onions are used, first slice the onions in half lengthwise before slicing crosswise. An electric slicer offers a great advantage when preparing a large quantity of sliced shallots or onions. Fry the sliced shallot pieces in hot oil in a wok over moderately low heat for 5-7 minutes. The amount of oil used for frying should be at least the same as the amount of shallots. Stir frequently so they brown evenly. When the slices turn a light tan and rise up to the top remove them quickly from the oil with a slotted spoon. Place the flakes on paper towels for 15 minutes until they cool enough to become crispy, then store immediately. When stored in a sealed container or plastic bag in the refrigerator or freezer, fried shallots will last for a long time. Fried garlic is prepared in the same manner.

Coconut: the indispensable ingredient

Indonesia is one of the world's largest producers of coconuts. There the coconut palm is "the tree of life" since every part of the tree finds its use. The most precious part of the tree of course is the fruit, which is produced year round. The meat of the young fruit makes a refreshing snack. Milk or cooking oil is extracted from the ripe, mature coconut. The toddy or sap that flows from the inflorescence of the coconut palm can be drunk fresh or fermented to make a sweetish alcoholic drink called *tuak*. The fresh leaves are used for decoration and shade throughout the villages at parties and weddings. When dry, the vein of the leaf becomes hard and stiff and can be easily separated from the leaf using a knife. These veins, which are about half yard long, are used to make rakes. The fiber from the husk of the fruit has a lot of applications, such as brooms, brushes and ropes. The coconut shell is used for making ladles (usually with bamboo handles) or other utensils. The trunk of the coconut palm can be used to build bridges, small crafts and temporary shelters.

In many places in Indonesia young coconuts are sold by the side of the road. The vendor will make a small hole on top of the nut and insert a straw into the hole so that the water can be drunk straight from the shell. The coconut water has a refreshing sweet taste and is a fantastic thirst quencher. After the water has been consumed, the vendor will break the nut open so that the young tender meat can be scraped out with a spoon. When used for this purpose, it is important to select a coconut at exactly the right maturity. If the nut is too young, the meat is too thin and there is too little to scrape out, but if the nut is too ripe, the meat is too fibrous and hard. Another popular way to serve young coconut meat is as a refreshing drink by mixing it with coconut water, syrup and shaved ice. Young coconuts with tender and moist meat are not easy to find in the United States. However, plastic bags of frozen slivers of young coconut meat are sold in some Asian markets.

Coconut water should not be mistaken for coconut milk, which is the liquid extract of the meat of mature coconuts. Coconut milk is indispensable in Indonesian cuisine. It is used in sauces, soups, rice and desserts. In Indonesia coconut milk is always prepared fresh shortly before use. As described below, most will agree that it is too tedious to prepare fresh coconut milk. Fortunately, ready-made coconut milk in cans is available in all Asian markets and in many specialty food stores. The recipes in this book use canned coconut milk, as I believe that most Americans will prefer to use canned coconut milk for convenience. Shake the can before opening to mix the content. For cooking it is important to avoid using a sweetened product, which is used mainly for making sweet desserts and beverages.

Before the coconut is cracked open, the liquid is drained out by punching holes in the three brown coconut eyes. To loosen the meat from the outer shell, the circumference of the nut is repeatedly rapped with the dull back edge of a cleaver. Another way is to heat the unopened nut either over a flame or in the oven at 250°F for 30-60 minutes. A few firm hits will crack the shell of the nut and open it.

Coconut meat has a thin brown skin that can be peeled off with a knife or potato peeler. Traditionally, the coconut meat is grated with a hand grater. Then an equal amount of lukewarm water is added. The mixture is kneaded for about 2 minutes, then squeezed and strained to produce a thick coconut milk. This process is repeated using the drained grated coconut meat. The second pressing produces coconut milk that is less thick and creamy. Alternatively, an electrical blender can be used. The coconut meat is cut into small pieces and blended with lukewarm water. The blended mixture is squeezed and strained to obtain the milk.

UTENSILS

The wok (*kuali or wajan*): the versatile pan

It is entirely possible to cook Indonesian dishes with ordinary American utensils. But if there is one utensil that makes cooking of Indonesian foods simpler, it is a wok. A wok is an all-purpose cooking pan and can be found in all Indonesian kitchens.

A wok is a large cooking pan with a round bottom and gently sloping sides. The unique shape of the pan allows easy stirring of the food. Since the heat concentrates in the center and evenly radiates outward, a quick cooking is possible. The wok is also excellent for deep-frying since its round bottom reduces the amount of oil required and its depth prevents the usual spattering of the oil.

Traditionally woks are made of carbon steel, cast iron or stainless steel, but woks with a nonstick Teflon layer are now available. A new iron wok needs to be seasoned to prevent food contents from sticking and to avoid a metallic flavor in the food. The seasoning, which should be repeated several times in order to be effective, includes washing with hot water and soap, greasing with cooking oil over the entire surface, heating for about a minute, followed by rinsing with hot water. It should be dried immediately after washing, then it should be greased with cooking oil to prevent rusting. Teflon-coated woks do not need the pretreatment described above, but require a special care for preventing scratches.

Mortar and pestle (*cobek or ulekan*): the traditional grinder

Indonesians generally buy whole or fresh spices and then grind them shortly before use. The initial preparation of the spice mixture is a unique feature of Indonesian cooking. The authentic way of grinding and mashing spices is to use a *cobek*, which is a mortar and pestle. Indonesian cooks prefer to use a *cobek* to an electric blender to get the desired size and structure of the ground ingredients.

The mortar has a saucer shape and is made of stone or clay. The pestle has a handle carved at a right angle to the head and is made of stone or wood. A stone mortar goes with a stone or wooden pestle, whereas a clay mortar is only used in combination with a wooden pestle. The Indonesian shallow mortar and crooked pestle are distinctively shaped from the deep mortar and straight pestle used by the Chinese, Thai and Malaysians. Consequently, Indonesian cooks grind their ingredients using a forwards and backwards motion across the mortar, while the Chinese cooks use a pounding motion.

The cleaver: the all-purpose knife

A cleaver (with a blade of 3-4 inches deep) is useful not only for chopping boned meat, but is also handy for mincing meat or seafood, chopping or finely slicing meat or vegetables, and slapping spices with the flat side (to release the flavor of ginger or lemongrass or to remove the skin of garlic).

The silverware: the tools from hand to mouth

In Indonesia the only utensils set on the table are forks and spoons, while knives are absent. The fork is held in the left hand and the spoon in the right. The fork guides the food neatly onto the spoon. Meat and vegetables are often served bite-size or cooked sufficiently tender to be shredded with a fork and spoon. Even when larger pieces of food — like whole fish, prawn, duck or chicken — are served, these are also cut with a spoon or fork. Duck or chicken pieces may be picked up by the hand. When shrimp or prawns are served inside the shell, it is acceptable to peel them with one's hands. For noodles chopsticks are sometimes used.

In villages, most Indonesians like to eat with the fingers of their right hand, although spoons are provided to transfer the food to the individual plates. The left hand is considered unclean. A finger bowl is usually provided to moisten the fingers before eating so that the rice will not stick to them. The food is formed into small balls with the fingers, but no trace of food should touch the palm of the hand. The proper way to insert the food into the mouth is by not allowing the fingers themselves to enter the mouth.

Rice Noodles

Noodles

Lime

Tamarind

Chilies

Shallots

Candle Nuts

Galangal

Garlic

Ginger

Star Anise

Coriander

Lemon Grass

Tamarind

Cloves

Cumin

Lime Leaves

Turmeric

Cinnamon

INGREDIENTS, SPICES, AND SUBSTITUTES

The word spice is of French origin, meaning "fruit of the earth." Indonesian food is unique in its imaginative use of spices. Many of the spices used in Indonesian foods can now be found in well-stocked supermarkets. Most spices also find their applications as medicinal remedies. The English names precede the Indonesian names, which are printed in italics. In some cases the Latin names are also given. In the spelling for Indonesian words, the letters have about the same sound. The vowels *a*, *o*, *i* and *u* are pronounced as in the words f*a*r, h*o*b, s*ee*n and p*u*t, respectively. The vowel *e* when stressed is pronounced as the *e* in l*e*t and when unstressed as the *a* in *a*mong. Most of the consonants have a similar sound as in English. The *c*, however, is pronounced like *ch* in the word *ch*air. The *g* is spoken like the *g* in *g*o. The Indonesian *h* is strongly pronounced when it is used at the front or middle of a word, but is nearly silent at the end of a word.

Agar *(agar–agar)*. Agar-agar is a gelatinous colloidal extract of a mixture of red algae (*Rhodophyceae*). The algae are washed and dried, then the agar—part of the cell wall—is extracted with boiling water, forming a gel as it cools. The gel is a complex mixture of polysaccharides. Agar-agar is transparent, odorless and tasteless. It is slowly soluble in hot water, but insoluble in cold water. It has long been used by Asians for making jellies and in other food preparations.

Bamboo shoots *(rebung)*. Only the shoots of very young bamboo are used. They are collected before they appear above the ground. When obtained fresh they need to be boiled for a long time. They are available already cooked and ready-to-use in Asian markets. Bamboo shoots sold in cans are nearly as good as the freshly cooked ones, but less crispy.

Beancurd *(tahu)*. Beancurd, also known as bean cake or tofu, is a soft, white, cheese-like cake. The Chinese beancurd, which is more suitable for Indonesian dishes, has a firmer texture than the Japanese version. Originating in China about 2000 years ago, it is now used extensively in most Asian cooking. It is available in Asian markets and well-stocked supermarkets.

Bean sprouts *(kecambah* or *tauge)*. Bean sprouts are white shoots sprouted from mung beans or soybeans. Fresh bean sprouts are available in Asian Markets and well-stocked supermarkets.

Candlenut *(kemiri)*: Aleurites triloba. Candlenut is used to add texture, oily consistency and a faint flavor. They can be substituted with macadamia nuts or raw cashews. Candlenut will last longer when stored cool.

Chayote *(labu Siam)*: Sechium edule. The chyote plant is a member of the gourd and melon family. It is native to southern Mexico and Central America. The flattened pear-shaped ripe fruit varies in color from whitish to dark green and has a taste and texture similar to summer squash. Each fruit contains one seed.

Large chili *(cabai besar)*: Capsicum annuum and small chili *(cabai rawit)*: Capsicum frutescens. The types of chilies used in Indonesia range from the tiny ones about _ inch long to the larger ones about 4-5 inches long. The color changes from green to red as the chilies ripen. The red ones are stronger in flavor and hotness.

Cinnamon *(kayu manis)*: Cinnamomum spp. The spice cinnamon is the inner bark of the trees of the genus Cinnamomum. Cinnamomum cassia is native to Indonesia and China. Cinnamomum zeylanicum is native to India and Sri Lanka. The aromatic reddish-brown inner barks tend to curl after being peeled off from the bark. The oil, distilled from the shoots and bark, is used to flavor candy, perfumes and medicines.

Cloves *(cengkeh)*: Syzygium aromaticum. Cloves are the fragrant tack-like flower buds of the tree that is native to the Moluccas (the Spice Islands of Indonesia). Ironically, cloves are not used very often in Indonesian cooking. However, large amounts of cloves are used in the tobacco industry. They are ground and mixed with tobacco to make the popular cigarette called *rokok kretek*. The oil of cloves is a powerful antiseptic and is frequently used as a local anesthetic for toothaches as well as in perfumes, blends of spices, medications and candies.

Coconut milk *(santan).* Coconut milk is not the liquid inside the nut, but the extract from the mature coconut meat. It is the basis of many Indonesian dishes. Canned coconut milk is used throughout the recipes in this cookbook. Leftover coconut milk can be frozen. The milk will separate into two layers upon thawing and has to be mixed thoroughly before use.

Coriander *(ketumbar)*: Coriandrum sativum. Coriander seed is one of the basic ingredients in Indonesian cuisine. The round seeds are actually the fruit of the plant. The seed has a completely different flavor and application from the leaf, known as cilantro or Chinese parsley. Therefore the seeds and leaves cannot be used interchangeably. Ground coriander is obtained from the seeds. The leaves and stems are frequently used in Thai and Mexican cooking.

Cumin *(jintan)*: Cuminum cyminum. Cumin is used in many Indonesian dishes, often in conjunction with coriander. It should be used sparingly because its strong aroma can dominate the flavor of the dish. The seeds are the part used as the spice.

Fish sauce *(kecap ikan).* Fish sauce is a thin, clear, brown and salty liquid extract of fermented seafood (usually fish) and is most commonly sold in bottles. Fish sauce delivers a fine aroma and taste and is a popular ingredient throughout Southeast Asia.

Five Spices powder *(rempah).* The powder consists of a mixture of approximately equal proportions of finely ground star anise, cinnamon, fennel, pepper and cloves. It is a brown-red powder with a sweet and fragrant aroma and tangy taste.

Galangal *(laos* or *langkuas)*: Alpinea galanga. Galangal is a member of the ginger family. It is highly aromatic, but less sharp in flavor than ginger. Galangal is one of the most widely used spices in Indonesian dishes. Powdered galangal can be substituted for fresh (1 teaspoon ground = 1 inch).

Garlic *(bawang putih)*: Allium sativum. The garlic plant originally grew in middle Asia where it has been cultivated for at least 5000 years. The therapeutic uses of garlic are at least as old as its use in food. Researchers have recently found that garlic has germicidal properties, can lower blood cholesterol levels if consumed at about 2 oz. (56 g) daily, and may prevent heart disease and stroke. Garlic is used as seasoning in the majority of Indonesian dishes. Sometimes it is deep-fried or stir-fried prior to use.

Ginger *(jahe)*: Zingiber officinale. A ginger plant grows 2-3 feet high, with long, narrow leaves and pale green flowers. The plant is native to southeastern Asia. Ginger is grown for the rhizome or enlarged underground stem is commonly referred to as the "root." The irregularly shaped root has a pale yellow color, a sweet and pungent aroma, and a sharp, spicy and tangy taste. It has been used in India and China since ancient times. For cooking it is advisable not to substitute fresh ginger with the dried or ground form. Fresh ginger is readily available in supermarkets. When kept dry and wrapped in the refrigerator, the root can last for at least a month. In Indonesia ginger is also an ingredient in sweet drinks and many kinds of snacks. The drink is made by boiling ginger, palm sugar, cloves and cinnamon sticks in water.

Glutinous rice *(ketan).* Glutinous rice *(ketan)* is sticky when cooked and is used primarily in sweet snacks or desserts. It is also called sticky rice or sweet rice.

***Kencur*: Cemeheria galanga.** *Kencur* is sometimes known as zedoary or cuthery. The root, which has a unique, camphor-like flavor is the part used as the spice. It is usually used sparingly because of its pungent taste. It is left out of the recipes in this book because it is not essential for the selected recipes.

Lemongrass *(sereh)*: Cymbopogon citratus. Lemongrass stalks are about 8-10 inches long, but only the bottom 6 inches of the stalks are used. In Indonesian cooking, lemongrass is used as a whole or sliced stalk. The tough fibrous outer leaves are removed and the stalk is crushed before use with a pestle or the edge of a cleaver to release the fragrance. It should be removed from the dish before serving. This fragrant herb is used to impart a lemony flavor to soups, seafood and meat dishes and spice pastes. Fresh lemongrass is available in Asian markets and well-stocked supermarkets. Powered lemongrass can be substituted for fresh (1 teaspoon ground = 1 fresh stalk).

Lime (jeruk limau): Citrus aurantifola. The fruit is spherical and has a green color which turns yellow when it is ripe. Limes impart a zesty and tart flavor into foods. Lemon may be used as a substitute. The lime tree originated in India. It was brought to Egypt by the Arab traders sometime before 900 AD It was introduced to Spain in the 13th century. Limes are a good source of potassium, vitamin C and bioflavonoids.

Lime leaf (daun jeruk): Citrus hystrix. If lime leaves are unavailable, one leaf can be replaced by a square inch of lemon peel. A lime leaf is used whole and removed from the dish before serving.

Noodles. The noodles used in Indonesian cooking are Chinese style, made from wheat, wheat and egg, rice or mung beans. They are available in Asian markets either fresh or dried, except rice vermicelli and mung bean thread noodles, which are sold only dried. Fresh noodles can be stored in the refrigerator for up to a week or frozen for a long time. Wheat noodles have a beige color and wheat-egg noodles have a slightly yellow color. Both wheat and wheat-egg noodles are available in medium (spaghetti- or fettucini-size) and thin (angel hair-size) widths and can be used for stir-frying, deep-frying or soups. Rice vermicelli noodles are wiry, thin and brittle. They can be stir-fried or used in soups after being softened in water or deep-fried in oil without pre-soaking. Mung bean thread noodles are wiry, thin, transparent and tough to cut before being rehydrated. They are also called transparent, cellophane or glass noodles. They are stir-fried or used in soups after being rehydrated.

Nutmeg (pala): Myristica fragrans. The spice nutmeg is the kernel of the fruit of the nutmeg tree which is native to the Moluccas (the Spice Islands of Indonesia), but is now cultivated in other tropical areas. Although native to Indonesia, nutmeg is not used very often in Indonesian cooking. The fleshy covering of the hard nut is usually pickled and eaten as a snack.

Onion (bawang Bombay): Allium cepa. It is believed that onions originated in Asia and have been cultivated since ancient times. Onions are characteristic for their pungent taste, which disappears when they are cooked. Onions are not used as much as shallots in Indonesian cooking.

Oyster sauce (saus tiram). Oyster sauce is a thick brown sauce made from oysters cooked in soy sauce and brine. It has a delicate aroma and taste. Oyster sauce is available in bottles and should be kept refrigerated once the bottle is opened.

Palm sugar (gula aren or gula Jawa): Arenga saccharifera. Palm sugar is made from the sap of palm flowers. The sap is boiled down to syrup, which is then dried into a cylindrical form. The sugar has an intense caramel flavor. It is sold in some Asian markets as square or round dark brown cakes. Since palm sugar may not be readily available, dark brown sugar is used instead in these recipes.

Pepper (merica): Piper nigrum. Pepper is the dried fruit of a vine that is native to Java. The search for pepper was the driving force for the European expedition in the 15th century to Indonesia. Black peppercorns are the dried ripe berries with the skin intact, while white peppercorns have had the dark hull removed. White pepper has a milder flavor. Both black and white pepper may be used for Indonesian cooking.

Salam leaf (daun salam): Eugeneia polyantha. *Salam* leaf is the leaf of a *salam* tree, which grows wild in Indonesia. Unfortunately, the leaf is not available in the United States. It is left out of the recipes in this cookbook because there is no substitute for it. Fortunately, missing *salam* leaf will not significantly impair the taste of the dish. Some cookbooks suggest a bay leaf as a substitute, although I find that this bears no resemblance to the taste of *salam* leaf.

Scallion (daun bawang): Allium fistulosum. The scallion is also called green onion or spring onion. It is actually the immature stage of onions. The leafy green tops along with the white bottom part are used for garnishing and flavoring.

Sesame oil (minyak sesam): Sesamum indicum. Sesame oil is an extract of sesame seeds. The seeds contain about 50% oil and 25% protein. The oil is used in small amounts as a seasoning or flavoring agent. Due to the presence of natural antioxidants, sesame oil is the most stable vegetable oil. It will keep for years without turning rancid.

Shallot *(bawang merah)*: Allium ascalonicum. The shallot is a member of the lily family and has a flavor similar to an onion, but forms a cluster of bulbs instead of a single one. It is believed to have originated in Central Asia. Shallots are sliced and eaten raw with *sambal* or added during cooking as a seasoning. Sometimes they are deep-fried or stir-fried prior to use. One shallot may be replaced by half of a medium size onion.

Shrimp paste (*terasi*). Shrimp paste has a powerful aroma and is used in small amounts as a basic flavoring agent in Indonesian cuisine. It is made from fermented salted shrimp or other seafood. In Indonesia, *terasi* is sold in the form of dry square bricks, whereas in the United States it is available in Asian markets in the form of a mushy wet paste kept in jars. *Terasi* will last for years when kept tightly sealed in the refrigerator.

Soy sauce *(kecap asin).* Soy sauce is a fermented soybean extract combined with salt. Soy sauce is available in light and dark versions. The light one is the most delicately flavored. The dark one derives its color from added caramel. Soy sauce has a fragrant and meaty aroma and a delicate salty taste. It is available in bottles and can be kept at room temperature for years. The Chinese light soy sauce, rather than the Japanese type, is preferred for Indonesian cooking.

Star anise: Illicium verum. Star anise is the dried fruit of a small evergreen tree that is native to China. The fruit consists of eight carpels arranged like a star, with a single seed in each one. It has a slightly bitter and pungent flavor and is one of the ingredients used in five-spices powder.

Sweet rice *(ketan):* see glutinous rice

Sweet soy sauce *(kecap manis).* Sweet soy sauce, which is typical of Indonesia, is made from dark soy sauce, molasses and brown sugar. Sometimes other spices — such as galangal, coriander or star anise — are also added. In some places in the United States sweet soy sauce may be hard to find. Therefore in my recipes a mixture of soy sauce and white or brown sugar has been used as a substitute.

Tamarind *(asam)*: Tamarindus indica. Tamarind trees grow wild in Indonesia. The leaves *(daun asam)* are boiled in water and drunk as a tonic, which is called *jamu*. The fruit exists in the form of 4-6 inch pods, which become brown when mature. Inside the shell of the pod are several hard, dark brown seeds in a row surrounded by brown soft meat. The meat is distinctive for its tangy and sour taste and is used for many purposes: candy, snack, drink, medicine and cooking. In this book, tamarind is replaced by lime or lemon juice because in some places in the United States tamarind may be hard to find.

Turmeric *(kunir* or *kunyit)*: Curcuma longa. Turmeric is a member of the ginger family and is native to Southeast Asia. The root is smaller and more intensely yellow than the ginger root. Fresh turmeric may be hard to find in the United States, but ground turmeric can be obtained in any Asian market (1 inch fresh root = 1-teaspoon ground tumeric). Indonesians usually use the small side roots that branch off because the taste is more flavorful and delicate. However the commercial ground turmeric includes the whole root.

Appetizers

Sweet Rice Filled with Chicken
Fried Plantain
Fried Springroll
Lamb Turnover
Crispy Stuffed Potatoes
Crispy Ragout
Crispy Ragout Pocket
Shrimp Snacks
Stuffed Vegetables and Calamari
Wonton and Siomai

Sweet Rice Filled with Chicken
Lemper

Ingredients

Filling

1	lb. chicken (or ¾ lb. boneless chicken)
½	cup coconut milk (shake can)
1	cup water
1	lime leaf (or 1 square inch lemon peel)
1	tbs. fried shallots
½	tsp. ground coriander
¼	tsp. ground cumin
¼	tsp. shrimp paste
1	tsp. fried garlic
½	tsp. sugar
½	tsp. salt

Sweet rice

1½	lbs. sweet rice
¼	cup coconut milk (shake can)
4	cups water
½	tsp. salt

Wrapping

Banana leaves (available frozen in Oriental grocery stores). Plastic wrap or aluminum foil can be used as a substitute.

Preparation

Filling

- Bring water in a pot to a boil
- Add chicken and other ingredients; cook 15 minutes
- Discard lime leaf or lemon peel
- Shred chicken finely; add to broth
- Simmer until all liquid is absorbed; stir occasionally to prevent burning

Sweet rice

- Soak sweet rice in water for 1 hour
- Drain; place in a heatproof container
- Add salt and coconut milk; mix
- Steam 30 minutes

Wrapping

- Clean banana leaves with a wet towel
- Cut leaves into 5½ x 3 inch and 9 x 1½ inch rectangles
- Layer rice ¼ inch thick; cut into 3½ x 2½ inch pieces
- Place a piece of rice onto each 5 ½ x 3 inch banana leaf section
- Spread 1 tbs. filling lengthwise along the center of the rice
- Fold both sides of rice toward each other, pressing firmly to make a roll
- Close the two ends to make a firmly packed rice roll
- Wrap the 5½ x 3 inch leaf around the roll; pin the ends with a toothpick
- Wrap the ends of the roll with a 9x1½ inch leaf; pin the ends with a toothpick.

Serving

- Serve at room temperature as an appetizer or snack.
- Makes 18 pieces

Fried Plantain
Pisang Goreng

Ingredients
2   overripe plantains (characterized by black skin)
1   egg
¼   cup all-purpose flour
½   cup cornstarch
¾   tbs. sugar
¼   tsp. salt
¼   cup water
2   cups vegetable oil
6   tbs. honey (optional)

Preparation
• Peel plantains; slice in half and cut each half into 3 pieces
• Prepare a smooth batter by mixing all ingredients, except plantains, honey, and oil
• Heat oil in a wok or frying pan
• Dip plantain pieces into batter
• Using a spoon, scoop each piece and slide it carefully into the hot oil
• Deep-fry over medium heat 1½ to 2 minutes per side

Serving
• Serve as an appetizer, dessert, or snack
• Serve warm or at room temperature. Serve warm with honey (optional). Honey and warm fried plantain offer a delightful combination.
• Makes 12 pieces

Did you know?
• Plantain appears to have originated on the Malay Peninsula. Plantain has a higher starch content but a lower sugar content than ordinary bananas. It is an excellent source of potassium.

Fried Springroll
Lumpia Goreng

Ingredients
Filling
1　lb. ground pork
¼　lb. cabbage
¼　lb. shrimp
3　cloves garlic
1½ cups bamboo shoots, julienne
2　cups bean sprouts
2　tbs. vegetable oil
3　tbs. soy sauce
1　tbs. sugar
½　tsp. ground pepper
2　tsp. salt

Sauce
1　piece (½ inch) fresh ginger
¼　cup water
1　tbs. cornstarch
3　tbs. vinegar
2　tbs. sugar
1　tsp. ground chili *(sambal)*
Dash salt

Wrapping & Frying
1　egg white
1　package springroll sheets
2　cups vegetable oil

Preparation
Filling
- Peel garlic and shrimp; chop
- Cut cabbage into thin slices
- Wash bamboo shoots, bean sprouts, and cabbage; drain well
- Heat oil in a wok or pan
- Stir-fry garlic 1 minute
- Add pork; stir-fry until cooked
- Add all other ingredients; stir-fry 1 minute

Sauce
- Peel and slice ginger
- Mix cornstarch with 1 tbs. water
- Mix all ingredients in a small pot; cook 2 minutes

Wrapping & Frying
- If frozen, thaw springroll sheets
- Place 1 springroll sheet on a flat plate
- Put 1½ tbs. filling on one edge of sheet
- Roll sheet tightly twice over the filling, fold in the ends to close them; roll again and seal the seam with egg white
- Heat oil in a wok or frying pan
- Deep-fry over medium heat until crispy and golden brown

Serving
- Serve hot with sauce as an appetizer or snack
- Makes 20 rolls

Lamb Turnover
Martabak

Ingredients

Filling

½ lb. lamb (or goat meat)
1 onion
1 leek
4 eggs
½ tsp. ground coriander
½ tsp. ground turmeric
¼ tsp. ground pepper
¼ tsp. ground cumin
2 tsp. garlic powder
¼ tsp. ground clove
½ tsp. salt

Wrapping & Frying

12 springroll sheets
½ cup vegetable oil

Preparation

Meat filling

- Grind lamb/goat meat
- Beat eggs lightly with a fork; save 2 tsp. for wrapping
- Peel onion and garlic; chop
- Wash and cut leek into thin slices
- Prepare filling by mixing all ingredients

Wrapping & Frying

- Place 3 tbs. filling in the middle of a spring roll sheet; fold the edges to meet in the middle, forming a 5 x 2½ inch rectangle; seal the seams with egg liquid
- Heat 2 tbs. oil in a nonstick pan
- Cook rolls 1½ minutes each side

Serving

- Serve hot or warm as a snack, appetizer, or dessert. Martabak is crispy on the outside, but moist and soft inside.
- Best served immediately but can be reheated in an oven or on a skillet
- Makes 12 pieces

Tip

Springroll sheets may be replaced with wonton sheets. Place 1 tbs. meat filling on a square of wonton sheet. Place another wonton sheet on top of the filling and press the edges with a fingertip. Cook small *martabak* as described above.

Crispy Stuffed Potatoes
Kroket Kentang

Ingredients
Filling

½   lb. ground beef
1   stalk parsley leaves
1   carrot (medium)
½   small onion
½   tbs. cornstarch
½   tbs. margarine
1   tbs. soy sauce
¼   tsp. ground nutmeg
½   tsp. sugar
¼   tsp. salt
dash pepper

Potato mix

1 ½ lbs. potatoes
½   cup dehydrated potato flakes
1   egg
2   tbs. margarine
2   tbs. dried milk
¼   tsp. ground pepper
½   tsp. ground nutmeg
1   tsp. salt

Frying

1   egg
2   tbs. milk
1   cup bread crumbs
2   cups vegetable oil

Preparation
Potato mix

• Steam potatoes until cooked
• Peel potatoes; mash while warm
• Add all ingredients; mix well

Filling

• Peel carrot and onion; chop
• Wash and chop parsley leaves
• Heat margarine in a small pan
• Stir-fry onion 1 minute
• Add beef and carrot; stir-fry 2 minutes
• Add the rest of the ingredients; stir-fry 2
  minutes

Stuffing and frying

• Make a ball with 2 tbs. potato mix
• Press the ball to form a pocket
• Add ¾ tbs. filling in the pocket
• Close the pocket to make a roll
• Mix egg and milk; beat lightly
• Coat rolls with egg, then bread crumbs
• Heat oil in a wok or frying pan
• Deep-fry over medium heat 1½-2
  minutes on each side

Serving
• Serve as a snack, appetizer, or dessert. Makes 16 pieces

Tips
• Potatoes taste better when steamed or boiled with the peels. Potatoes can be more easily
  peeled and mashed when warm.
• Adding the dehydrated potato flakes gives a better texture to the potato mix and prevents
  it from being too soggy which could cause it to break up when deep-fried.

Crispy Ragout
Kroket

Ingredients

Dough

1   lb. beef
4   oz. margarine or butter
1   cup all-purpose flour
5   cups water
1   tbs. Worcestershire sauce
1   tsp. ground pepper
¼   tsp. ground clove
1½ tsp. salt

Breading & Frying

1   egg
2   tbs. milk
1   cup bread crumbs

Preparation

Dough

- Cut meat into cubes
- Simmer meat and spices in a covered pot 1 hour or until meat is tender
- Shred meat finely; set aside broth
- Melt butter in a saucepan
- Turn heat off
- Add flour; mix to form a stiff dough
- Add beef and 3 cups broth while stirring (add broth gradually or the sauce will become lumpy)
- Cook until texture is stiff
- Let it cool, then refrigerate 1 hour

Breading & Frying

- Roll the dough into rolls 4-5 inches long and 1 inch wide or balls of 1-inch diameter
- Coat with breadcrumbs
- Refrigerate 30 minutes
- Mix egg and milk
- Dip meat rolls and balls in egg mixture and bread again
- Deep-fry in a wok or frying pan over medium heat 2-3 minutes or until brown
- Deep-fry in a wok or frying pan over medium heat 2-3 minutes or until brow

Serving

- Makes 15 rolls and 15 balls
- Serve with mustard-relish mixture and pickles

Did you know?

This recipe is of Dutch origin, but has become a common Indonesian snack.

Crispy Ragout Pocket
Rissoles

Ingredients

Filling

¾ lb. chicken with bones (or ½ lb. boneless)
1 small carrot
1 onion
¼ cup all-purpose flour
1 cup water
3 tbs. butter or margarine
1 tbs. sugar
½ tsp. ground nutmeg
½ tsp. ground pepper
1 tsp. salt

Pancake

2 eggs
¼ lb. butter or margarine
¾ cup all-purpose flour
¼ cup water
1 cup milk
2 tbs. cornstarch
1 tsp. salt

Frying

1 egg
2 tbs. milk
2 cups bread crumbs
1½ cups vegetable oil

Preparation

Filling

- Simmer chicken 20 minutes; cut into small pieces
- Peel onion and carrot; chop
- Heat butter. Stir-fry onion and carrot
- Gradually add flour and broth; mix
- Add the rest of the ingredients
- Cook 5 minutes while stirring

Pancake

- Mix all ingredients (except butter) until smooth
- Heat 1 tbs. butter in a 6 inch nonstick pan; pour 2 tbs. batter into pan; lift and rotate pan to spread the batter
- Cook 1 minute over medium heat
- Repeat for the rest of the batter

Wrapping and frying

- Mix egg and milk; beat lightly
- Place 2 tbs. filling 1½ inches from one side of each pancake
- Fold in the side and ends, forming a 3 x 1½ inch roll; seal seams with egg mixture
- Coat filled pancake with egg mixture, then bread crumbs
- Heat oil in a wok or frying pan
- Deep-fry filled pancakes over medium heat until golden brown and crispy

Serving

- Serve as an appetizer, dessert, or snack
- Makes 12 *rissoles*

Shrimp Snacks
Camilan Udang

Ingredients

Shrimp Mixture

1   lb. shrimp
2   oz. lard
1   piece (¼ inch) fresh ginger
1   egg white
1   scallion
2   tbs. all-purpose flour
1   tbs. cooking wine
2   tbs. cornstarch
½   tsp. ground pepper
1   tsp. salt

Omelet, wrap & frying

2   eggs
1   cup vegetable oil
3   sheets dry seaweed (8 x 8 inch)

Preparation

Shrimp mixture
- Grind lard and peeled shrimp
- Finely chop the white part of scallion
- Peel and finely grate ginger
- Mix all ingredients

Omelet filled with shrimp mixture
- Beat eggs lightly with a fork
- Make a thin omelet
- Spread 4 tbs. shrimp mixture on omelet
- Cover with an 8 x 8 inch seaweed sheet
- Spread a second shrimp layer
- Place 2 seaweed pieces of ½ x 8 inch each on opposite edges of the omelet
- Roll omelet from each of the two edges tightly until the two rolls meet in the middle; steam 4 minutes
- Cut into ¼ inch slices

Shrimp rolls
- Make shrimp mixture rolls the size of a little finger
- Wrap rolls with 1½ x 2½ inch seaweed sheets (shrimp mixture should stick out). Seal both ends using egg white
- Deep-fry rolls 1½ -2 minutes

Shrimp balls
- Place 3 tbs. of shrimp mixture in palm of left hand; close fingers to spurt a ball of shrimp mixture from the top of the fist
- With a spoon in right hand remove ball and drop it gently into the hot oil
- Deep-fry balls over medium heat 3-4 minutes or until crispy and golden brown

Serving
- Serve as an appetizer or snack; serve with chili sauce
- Makes 15 slices filled egg rolls, 15 pieces shrimp rolls and 20 pieces shrimp balls

Stuffed Vegetables and Calamari
Sayur Isi

Ingredients for

Filling
½ lb. ground pork
½ lb. shrimp
1   scallion
1   egg
1   tbs. sesame oil
2   tbs. fish sauce
1   tbs. soy sauce
¾ tsp. ground pepper
2   tsp. garlic powder

Vegetables & seafood
bell peppers
mushrooms
ripe tomatoes
cabbage
calamari

Preparation
• Wash, peel and grind shrimp
• Wash and chop scallion
• Break egg, remove shell
• Mix all ingredients thoroughly
• Remove the stems of mushrooms and the inside part of bell peppers and tomatoes
• Clean calamari
• Steam cabbage leaves 1 minute (This will make the leaves flexible)
• Fill vegetables and calamari with filling mix
• Steam until cooked

Serving
One pound of filling will stuff one small bell pepper, one tomato, one cabbage leaf, one calamari and two mushrooms.

Wonton and Siomai
Pangsit dan Siomai

Ingredients

Filling
Same as Stuffed Vegetables and Calamari

Others
1   package wonton wrappers (about 30 sheets; available in Oriental groceries)
1   scallion
2   cups chicken broth
½   cup vegetable oil
2   cups water
2   tsp. fried shallots

Preparation

Wrapping

- To wrap wonton, place wrapper on palm, spoon ½ tsp. filling in the center of wrapper, fold corner to corner to form a triangle, moisten the ends with water to seal, bring the widest 2 outer corners together so that the filled wonton folds up, then moisten with water so the ends stick together.
- To wrap siomai, place wrapper on palm, spoon 1 tbs. of filling mix in the center of wrapper, then fold wrapper up and pinch to the filling mix to form pleats. Tap siomai on a plate to make the bottom flat.

Frying

- Heat oil in a wok or frying pan
- Fry wonton over medium heat 2-3 minutes until light brown and crispy

Soup

- Boil wonton pieces in water 3 minutes
- Remove wonton pieces; discard water
- Wash and chop scallion
- Heat chicken broth
- Add wonton pieces to broth; sprinkle with scallion and fried shallots

Steaming

- Brush the bottom of the steamer with oil (to prevent sticking); place siomai pieces on it, leaving a ½-inch space between pieces
- Steam over medium heat 20 minutes

Serving
½ lb. filling makes 15 siomai pieces or 60 wonton pieces.

Soups

Vegetable Coconut Soup
Vegetable Soup with Filled Omelet
Chayote Soup
Asparagus Soup with Crab Meat
Tomato Chicken Soup with Vegetables
Chicken Noodle Soup
Curry Chicken Soup
Oxtail Tomato Soup
Oxtail Vegetable Soup

Vegetable Coconut Soup
Sayur Lodeh

Ingredients

3	lime leaves (or 3 square inches lemon peel)	¼	lb. string beans
1	large piece of beancurd (tofu)	½	cup coconut milk (shake can)
2	green chilies	1	cup vegetable oil
3	cloves garlic	4	cups water
3	candlenuts	1	tbs. ground galangal
1	chayote	1	tbs. sugar
2	shallots	½	tbs. salt
¼	lb. sliced bamboo shoots (from can)	¼	tsp. ground lemongrass
¼	lb. corn kernels (frozen or from can)	¼	tsp. ground coriander
¼	lb. baby corn (from can)	1	tsp. shrimp paste

Preparation

- Drain bamboo shoots; soak in water for 5 minutes and drain
- Peel chayote; julienne into 1½ x ½ x ½ inch strips
- Wash string beans and chilies; remove ends and chop into thirds
- Cut beancurd into 1½ x ½ x ½ inch pieces
- Heat oil in a wok or frying pan
- Deep-fry beancurd 5 minutes over high heat
- Peel shallots and garlic
- Grind shallots, garlic and candlenuts until smooth (add 4 tbs. water to facilitate grinding)
- Mix all spices with water and coconut milk in a pot; bring to a boil
- Add string beans, chilies and chayote
- Cover pot; simmer 5 minutes
- Add bamboo shoots, baby corn and corn kernels
- Cover pot; simmer 5 minutes

Serving

- Serves 5
- Can be served with rice

Tip

The dish will develop more flavorful when prepared a day ahead. Refrigerate and reheat at serving time.

Vegetable Soup with Filled Omelet
Kuah Sayur dan Telur Goreng Isi

Ingredients
½   lb. chicken with bones
1/8 lb. string beans
1/8 lb. cauliflower
1/8 lb. ham
4   mushrooms
1   carrot
2   eggs
4   cups water
5   tbs. ground meat (chicken, beef, or pork)
1   tbs. vegetable oil
1   tbs. fried shallots
1   tbs. salt
¼   tsp. ground pepper
1   tsp. fried garlic

Preparation
Filled Omelet
- Break eggs into a bowl
- Add dash of salt and pepper; beat lightly with a fork
- Add 2 tbs. beaten egg to ground meat; mix
- Heat oil in a nonstick pan
- Make a thin omelet using the remaining beaten egg
- Spread ground meat thinly over the omelet
- Roll omelet from one edge tightly to other edge; steam 3 minutes or until meat is cooked
- Slice filled omelet; set aside

Soup
- Bring water to a boil; add chicken
- Cover pot; simmer 8 minutes
- Cut chicken into small pieces; set aside
- Peel and cut carrot into slices
- Wash and cut string beans, cauliflower, and mushrooms into serving pieces
- Cut ham into slices
- Bring broth to a boil
- Add fried garlic, salt, pepper, string beans, and carrot
- Cover pot; simmer 5 minutes
- Add cauliflower, ham, and chicken pieces; cook 4 minutes
- Add mushrooms, omelet slices, and fried shallots before serving

Serves 4

Chayote Soup
Kuah Waluh

Ingredients
¼ lb. shrimp
½ lb. beef
1   chayote (¾ lb.)
1   scallion
3   cups water
1½ tbs. fried shallots
1   tbs. margarine
1   tbs. salt
¼ tsp. ground pepper
1   tsp. fried garlic
1   tsp. sesame oil

Preparation
• Cut beef into small square pieces
• Wash and chop scallion
• Peel chayote; cut into small pieces
• Wash and peel shrimp
• Heat margarine in a pan; stir-fry shrimp 1 minute
• Bring water in a pot to a boil
• Add beef gradually so that water continues boiling
• Cover pot; simmer 20-30 minutes
• Add chayote, fried garlic, salt, and pepper
• Cover pot; simmer 5 minutes
• Add fried shallots, scallion, shrimp, and sesame oil; cook 30 seconds

Serving
Serve as soup or main dish with rice for 2

Did you know?
Chayote is high in water (92%) and a source of potassium and vitamin C.

Asparagus Soup with Crab Meat
Kuah Asparagus

Ingredients
½ lb. chicken with bones
¼ lb. crab meat (imitation crab meat can be used as a substitute)
¼ lb. corn kernels (frozen)
4½ cups water
12 spears asparagus
1 egg
1 tbs. cooking wine
2 tbs. cornstarch
1 tbs. soy sauce
2 tbs. salt
¼ tsp. ground pepper
1 tsp. fried garlic
1 tsp. sesame oil

Preparation
• Wash asparagus, remove hard part of stems; cut into 1½ inch pieces; separate stem pieces from spears
• Tear crabmeat into thin slices
• Bring water in a pot to a boil
• Add chicken piece by piece so that water continues boiling
• Cover pot; simmer 10 minutes
• Cut chicken meat into small pieces; discard bones; set aside broth
• Mix cornstarch with 2 tbs. water
• Heat broth
• Add asparagus stems; cook 4 minutes
• Add spears; cook 4 minutes
• Add chicken, crabmeat, cornstarch solution, and all spices; stir
• Beat egg lightly with a fork
• Pour beaten egg slowly into the boiling soup and stir gently; cook 1 minute

Serves 6

Did you know?
Asparagus originated around the eastern Mediterranean. It is high in water (92%) and a good source of vitamin A. It also contains fair amounts of thiamin, riboflavin, and niacin.

Tomato Chicken Soup with Vegetables
Sup Merah

Ingredients

1 lb. chicken with bones	1½ tbs. fried shallots
3 smoked frankfurters	2 tbs. cornstarch
5 cups water	2 tbs. sugar
2 stalks celery	2 tbs. salt
¼ lb. smoked ham	¾ tsp. ground nutmeg
¼ lb. green peas (frozen)	½ tsp. ground pepper
¾ lb. ripe tomatoes	1½ tsp. fried garlic
¼ lb. string beans	
½ lb. carrots	

Preparation

- Wash and cut string beans into quarters
- Peel and slice carrots
- Wash and cut celery into slices
- Cut tomatoes into small pieces
- Cut frankfurters and ham into slices
- Mix cornstarch with 2 tbs. water
- Bring water in a pot to a boil
- Add chicken and tomatoes; cover pot; simmer 8 minutes
- Cut chicken meat into small pieces; discard bones; set aside broth
- Add string beans, carrots, fried garlic, fried shallots, salt, sugar, nutmeg and pepper; simmer 5 minutes
- Add celery, green peas, frankfurters, ham, and chicken pieces and cornstarch solution; cook 2 minutes

Serving
Serve with French bread for 5

Did you know?
Tomatoes contain about 94% water and high amounts of vitamins A and C. Ripe (red) tomatoes contain about 3 to 4 times as much vitamin A as mature green tomatoes. Canned tomatoes contain only about three-fourths the vitamin C content of fresh ripe tomatoes.

Chicken Noodle Soup
Kuah Mi Ayam

Ingredients

Noodles
½ lb. fresh Chinese wheat noodles
10 cups water
vegetable leaves, such as kai lan, optional

Broth
¼ lb. chicken bones
3 cups water
1 tsp. fried garlic
3 tsp. salt
dash pepper

Meat
½ lb. boneless chicken
2 cloves garlic
1 tbs. vegetable oil
1½ tbs. soy sauce
2 tsp. fried shallots
½ tsp. sesame oil
dash pepper

Preparation

Broth
- Bring water in a pot to a boil
- Add all ingredients for broth
- Cover pot; simmer 10 minutes
- Remove bones

Noodles
- Bring water to a boil; set aside 4 cups
- Add noodles; cook 1-2 minutes or until noodles are cooked; stir gently with a fork to separate noodles
- Drain noodles; rinse with tap water
- Rinse noodles with the reserved hot water

Meat
- Cut chicken meat into small pieces
- Peel and slice garlic
- Heat vegetable oil in a wok or pan
- Stir-fry garlic 1 minute
- Add chicken pieces; stir-fry until cooked
- Add soy sauce, sesame oil and pepper; stir-fry for a few seconds
- Sprinkle with fried shallots

Serving
- Place warm noodles in 2 bowls
- Put meat over noodles (with steamed vegetable leaves, optional)
- Pour hot broth over noodles shortly before serving
- Serves 2

Curry Chicken Soup
Soto Ayam

Ingredients

Broth & meat

3 chicken legs (2 lbs.) or any other part
2 cups water
2 lime leaves (or 2 square inches lemon peel)
1 piece (½ inch) fresh ginger
½ tbs. fried garlic
1 tbs. salt
¼ tsp. ground lemongrass
¼ tsp. ground coriander
½ tsp. ground turmeric
¼ tsp. ground pepper

Noodles & cabbage

2 cups hot water
1 scallion
½ lime
¼ lb. cellophane noodles
¼ lb. Savoy cabbage
1 tbs. fried shallots

Preparation

Broth & meat

- Peel and slice ginger
- Mix all ingredients for broth (except chicken) in a pot; bring to a boil
- Add chicken piece by piece so that broth continues boiling; cover pot
- Simmer 20 minutes
- Remove chicken; set aside broth
- Cut chicken into small pieces

Noodles & cabbage

- Soak cellophane noodles in hot water for 2 minutes
- Wash Savoy cabbage; cut into very thin slices

Serving

- Serve the chicken, hot broth, cellophane noodles, cabbage, and lime slices, along with some chili sauce separately on the table. Place some rice on a plate or in a bowl and add a portion of chicken, cellophane noodles, and cabbage over the rice. Ladle the hot broth over the top. Sprinkle fried shallots and chopped scallion and squeeze lime juice on top. Add chili sauce to taste.
- Serves 3

Oxtail Tomato Soup
Tomat Sup Buntut

Ingredients
2   lbs. oxtail (cut into 2 inch pieces)
1   lb. tomatoes
2½ cups water
1   carrot
2   tbs. fried shallots
2   tbs. brown sugar
1   tbs. fried garlic
3   tbs. soy sauce
1½ tbs. salt
½   tsp. crushed dried red chilies, adjust amount to taste
2   tsp. ground nutmeg
¼   tsp. ground pepper

Preparation
• Remove excess fat from oxtail
• Cut tomatoes into 8 equal wedges
• Mix all ingredients (except oxtail, carrot and fried shallots) with water in a pot
• Bring mixture to a boil
• Add oxtail piece by piece so that water continues boiling
• Cover pot; simmer 1¼ hours or until meat is tender
• Peel and cut carrot into large pieces
• Add carrot and fried shallots to broth
• Cover pot; simmer 10 minutes
• Remove oxtail pieces from broth
• Remove bones; add meat back to broth
• Reheat broth before serving

Serving
Serve with rice for 2

Tip to remove fat from liquid
Oxtail may contain excess fat that is difficult to trim off. The fat will dissolve in the broth upon cooking. The broth can be prepared in advance and refrigerated to let the fat congeal for easy removal.

Sweet Rice Filled with Chicken

Fried Spring rolls

Stuffed Vegetables and Calamari

Crispy Stuffed Potatoes

Shrimp Snacks

Asparagus Soup

Curry Chicken Soup

Fried Corn Patties

Bamboo Shoots in Coconut Sauce

Salad with Peanut Dressing

Fried Rice with Spicy Sausage

Crispy Rice Noodles

Fried Fish in Sweet & Sour Sauce

Fried Fish Cutlets in Curry Sauce

Sautéed Clams in Soy Sauce

Sautéed Prawns

Oxtail Vegetable Soup
Sup Buntut

Ingredients
2   lbs. oxtail pieces
¼   lb. string beans
¼   lb. cauliflower
5   cups water
1   stalk celery
2   carrots
1   tbs. fried shallots
¾   tsp. ground nutmeg
¼   tsp. ground pepper
1½ tsp. fried garlic
2½ tsp. salt

Preparation
- Remove excess fat from oxtail pieces
- Bring water and salt in a pot to a boil
- Add oxtail piece by piece so that water continues boiling
- Cover pot; simmer 1¼ hours or until meat is tender
- Remove bones; add meat back to broth
- Peel and cut carrots into thin slices
- Wash string beans; remove ends, then cut into thirds
- Wash cauliflower; cut into serving pieces
- Bring broth to a boil
- Add pepper, nutmeg, fried garlic and string beans
- Cover pot; simmer 5 minutes
- Add carrot, celery and cauliflower
- Cover pot; simmer 5 minutes

Serving
- Sprinkle with fried shallots before serving
- Serve as soup or as a main dish with rice
- Serves 4

Vegetables

Fried Corn Patties
Sautéed Vegetables with Beancurd
Bamboo Shoots in Coconut Sauce
Stuffed Chinese Eggplant
Salad with Peanut Dressing
Fried Cauliflower

Fried Corn Patties
Perkedel Jagung

Ingredients

Corn Patties

1	lb. frozen corn kernels
¼	lb. shrimp (optional)
1	onion
1	egg
2	tbs. all-purpose flour
2	tbs. cornstarch
1½	tsp. ground coriander
½	tsp. ground pepper
½	tsp. ground cumin
2	tsp. garlic powder
2	tsp. salt
1½	cups vegetable oil

Pickled Cucumbers

2	kirby cucumbers
2	shallots
½	cup water
2	tbs. white vinegar
½	tbs. sugar
½	tsp. salt

Preparation

Corn Patties

• Grind corn kernels coarsely
• Peel shrimp
• Mix all ingredients, except oil
• Heat oil in a wok or frying pan
• Scoop up the corn mixture with a spoon; slide the patty into the oil
• Deep-fry each side 1½ minutes

Pickled Cucumbers

• Peel cucumbers and shallots
• Remove cucumber seeds; cut cucumbers into sticks
• Cut shallots into slices
• Mix all ingredients
• Refrigerate 30 minutes

Serving

• Serve the corn patties as an appetizer or snack, or as a main dish with rice
• Serve pickled cucumber as an accompaniment
• Makes 24 patties

Tips

• Corn kernels are easier to grind when still frozen
• The temperature of the oil should be controlled. If the temperature is too high, the inside part of the patties will not cook well. If the temperature is too low, the patties will absorb too much oil.
• Pickled cucumbers are served as an accompaniment to many dishes. The light vinegar flavor and sweetness make pickled cucumbers an excellent palate refresher during the meal. The flavor is enhanced when prepared a few hours in advance. Whole or slices of green or red chilies may be added.

Sautéed Vegetables with Beancurd
Sambal Goreng Tahu

Ingredients

¼	lb. corn kernels (frozen or from can)	1	onion
¼	lb. sliced bamboo shoots (from can)	2	tbs. dark brown sugar
¼	lb. baby corn (from can)	1	tbs. ground galangal
½	lb. ground beef	2	tbs. soy sauce
¼	lb. string beans	1	tsp. shrimp paste
2	large pieces beancurd (tofu)	½	tsp. salt
3	chilies (red or green)	1	cup vegetable oil
3	cloves garlic		

Preparation

- Cut beancurd into 1 x ½ x ½ inch pieces
- Heat oil in a wok or nonstick pan
- Deep-fry beancurd 5 minutes over high heat
- Peel garlic and onion; cut into slices
- Wash string beans and chilies; remove ends and chop into thirds
- Heat 1 tbs. oil in a wok or pan
- Stir-fry onion and garlic 2 minutes
- Add ground beef, string beans, chilies and all spices; stir-fry 10 minutes
- Add bamboo shoots and baby corn; stir-fry 3 minutes
- Add corn kernels and beancurd; stir-fry 3 minutes

Serving
Serve with rice for 4

Did you know how to make tofu?
Soya beans are washed and soaked for 18 hours or until the beans are swollen. The steep water is discarded and fresh water is added at a ratio of water to beans of 10:1. The beans are then ground and filtered through double-layered cheesecloth. The liquid extract is boiled and cooled to 80° C (176° F), then magnesium sulfate or calcium sulfate solution is slowly added with gentle stirring. The curd is allowed to settle. When the temperature drops to 50° C, the curd is filtered through double layered cheesecloth. The liquid is discarded. A weight is placed on top of the curd to force more water out. The pressure placed onto the curd determines the hardness of the tofu.

Bamboo Shoots in Coconut Sauce
Sambal Goreng Rebung

Ingredients
½   cup coconut milk (shake can)
1½ cups sliced bamboo shoots (from can)
2   cups water
¼   lb. shrimp
¼   red bell pepper
1½ tbs. ground galangal
1½ tbs. fried shallots
½   tbs. fried garlic
1½ tbs. sugar
½   tsp. ground red chilies *(sambal)*, adjust amount to taste
½   tsp. shrimp paste
1½ tsp. salt

Preparation
• Drain bamboo shoots; soak in water for 5 minutes and drain
• Peel shrimp, leaving tails intact
• Wash and grind bell pepper in a food processor
• Make broth by boiling water in a pot with all ingredients, except shrimp and fried shallots
• Cover pot; simmer 10 minutes
• Add shrimp and fried shallots; cook 3 minutes

Serving
Serve with rice for 3

Stuffed Chinese Eggplant
Terung Isi

Ingredients

1 lb. Chinese eggplant
1½ cups vegetable oil

Batter

3 egg whites
7 tbs. cornstarch
4 tbs. water
½ tsp. salt

Stuffing

¼ lb. ground pork
¼ lb. shrimp
1 egg yolk
1 tbs. soy sauce
¼ tsp. ground pepper
1 tsp. garlic powder
1 tsp. salt

Preparation

• Peel and grind shrimp
• Mix all ingredients for stuffing; set aside
• Prepare batter by mixing all ingredients for batter; set aside
• Wash eggplants and cut diagonally into 1-inch sections
• Cut partially thorough each section, leaving the two thin slices attached
• Insert about ¾ tbs. stuffing mixture in between the eggplant slices
• Heat oil in a wok or frying pan
• Dip filled eggplant slices into batter; deep-fry 1-1½ minutes on each side over medium heat

Serving

• Serve as a snack or appetizer or with rice as a main dish
• Makes 20 pieces

Salad with Peanut Dressing
Gado-gado

Ingredients
Dressing

1¼ cups water
3 tbs. coconut milk (shake can)
3 tbs. chunky peanut butter
1 tbs. dark brown sugar
3 tbs. roasted peanuts
2 tbs. fried shallots
1 tbs. fried garlic
2 tbs. lime juice
1 tsp. ground red chilies *(sambal)*, adjust
   amount to taste
½ tsp. shrimp paste
dash coriander
dash salt

Salad

10 lettuce leaves (any kind)
1 Granny-Smith apple
½ cup alfalfa sprouts
½ cucumber
4 carrots
1 egg

Preparation
Dressing

- Grind roasted peanuts coarsely
- Mix all ingredients for dressing (except limejuice) in a small pot
- Bring to a short boil, stirring occasionally to prevent burning
- Add lime juice; mix

Salad

- Cut lettuce into ½ inch strips
- Shred carrots
- Peel and slice cucumber and apple
- Hard boil eggs; cool and slice
- Mix all salad ingredients

Serving
- Pour dressing on salad at room temperature shortly before serving
- Serves 4

Tip
The dressing can be prepared and refrigerated a few days in advance. The salad looks and tastes fresher when prepared immediately before serving, but may be prepared 1 day ahead and refrigerated. To prevent browning, before storage dip cut vegetables for a few seconds in water sprinkled lightly with lime or lemon juice. *Gado-gado* can be prepared with almost any combination of vegetables.

Fried Cauliflower
Kembang Kol Goreng

Ingredients
½ lb. cauliflower
1   egg
¼ cup water
6   tbs. all-purpose flour
2   tbs. cornstarch
½ tsp. ground pepper
1   tsp. salt
1½ cups vegetable oil

Preparation
• Wash and cut cauliflower into serving size pieces
• Prepare batter by mixing all ingredients, except cauliflower and oil
• Heat oil in a wok or frying pan to medium hot
• Dip cauliflower pieces into batter; carefully slide into the hot oil
• Deep-fry 2 minutes

Serving
• Serve as a snacks or appetizer, or as a main dish with rice
• Serve with chili sauce

Rice and Noodles

Fried Rice with Bacon
Ginger Fried Rice
Fried Rice with Shrimp
Fried Rice with Spicy Sausage
Curry Rice Noodles
Crispy Rice Noodles
Fried Noodles
Crispy Noodles

Fried Rice with Bacon
Nasi Goreng Bacon

Ingredients
2   cups cooked rice
¼   lb. bacon
1   chili (optional)
2   cloves garlic
2   scallions
1   shallot
2   tbs. fish sauce
2   tsp. sugar
½   tsp. salt
dash pepper

Preparation
- Cook rice at least 1 hour prior to use; allow to cool
- Wash and chop scallions and chili
- Peel shallot and garlic; slice into thin slices
- Cut bacon into ¾ inch slices
- Stir-fry bacon pieces in a wok or large nonstick frying pan
- Set aside bacon; leave 1 tbs. melted bacon fat in the wok or pan
- Add garlic and shallot; stir-fry 2 minutes
- Add rice, pepper, sugar, salt and fish sauce; mix thoroughly
- Stir-fry 2 minutes over medium heat (stirring constantly to prevent the rice from sticking to the pan)
- Add scallion and chili pieces; stir-fry 1 minute

Serving
Serves 2

Ginger Fried Rice
Nasi Goreng Jahe

Ingredients
2   cups cooked rice
¼   lb. ground pork
1   piece (2 inch) fresh ginger
2   cloves garlic
1   shallot
2   tbs. vegetable oil
3   tbs. fish sauce
2   tsp. sugar

Preparation
• Cook rice at least 1 hour prior to use; allow to cool
• Peel ginger; grate finely
• Peel garlic and shallot; cut into thin slices
• Heat oil in a wok or large nonstick pan
• Stir-fry garlic and shallot 1 minute
• Add ginger; stir-fry 1 minute
• Add ground pork; stir-fry 2 minutes
• Add rice, fish sauce, and sugar; mix completely
• Stir-fry 2 minutes over medium heat (stirring constantly to prevent the rice from sticking to the pan)

Serving
Serves 2

Memories
    This type of fried rice is an inspiration from my mother. I remember that one evening when my mother had an upset stomach, she prepared fried rice with ginger. Ginger is believed to soothe an upset stomach and is commonly used in Indonesia as a drink in combination with tea. My mother gave me some of the fried rice to taste. Although she has never prepared the dish again since then, the good pungent and aromatic flavor of the fried rice stayed in my memory. And now, many years later, I still feel nostalgic as I prepare this unique dish.

    The amount of the ginger used in this recipe is adjustable to personal preference. It is important to grate the ginger fine so that the taste is uniform throughout the rice. If you like ginger, you should try this recipe, experimenting with it several times to discover just the right amount of ginger for your taste.

Fried Rice with Shrimp
Nasi Goreng Udang

Ingredients
2   cups cooked rice
¼   lb. shrimp (small or medium size)
¼   lb. pork (or chicken or beef)
2   cloves garlic
1   shallot
2   tbs. vegetable oil
1   tsp. ground red chilies *(sambal)*, adjust amount to taste
1   tsp. brown sugar
1   tsp. salt

Preparation
• Cook rice at least 1 hour prior to use; allow to cool
• Cut meat into thin slices
• Peel shrimp; make a shallow cut along the back of each
• Peel garlic and shallot; cut into thin slices
• Heat oil in a wok or large nonstick pan
• Add garlic and shallots; stir-fry 2 minutes
• Add meat; stir-fry 2 minutes
• Add shrimp; stir-fry 1 minute
• Add rice and the remaining ingredients
• Stir-fry 2 minutes over medium heat (stirring constantly to prevent it from sticking to the pan)

Serving
Serves 2

Fried Rice with Spicy Sausage
Nasi Goreng Sosis

Ingredients
2   cups cooked rice
2   spicy sausages (¼ lb.): spicy Italian sausages can be used
2   cloves garlic
¼   lb. Savoy cabbage
1   tbs. vegetable oil
½   tbs. sugar
1½ tsp. salt

Preparation
- Cook rice at least 1 hour prior to use; allow to cool
- Peel garlic; cut into thin slices
- Cut sausages into thin slices
- Wash and cut Savoy cabbage into thin slices
- Heat oil in a wok or large nonstick pan
- Stir-fry garlic 1 minute
- Add sausage slices; stir-fry until cooked
- Add rice and the remaining ingredients
- Stir-fry the mixture 2 minutes over low heat (stirring constantly to prevent it from sticking to the pan)

Serving
Serves 2

Curry Rice Noodles
Bihun Kunir

Ingredients
½   lb. dried Chinese rice vermicelli
½   lb. meat (pork, chicken or beef)
¼   lb. Savoy cabbage
¼   lb. shrimp
2   cups bean sprouts
6   cups water
2   cloves garlic
¼   bell pepper
1   scallion
½   onion
½   tbs. ground turmeric
4   tbs. vegetable oil
4   tbs. fish sauce
¼   tsp. ground pepper
1   tsp. salt

Preparation
• Bring water in a pot to a boil; remove pot from stove
• Soak vermicelli in hot water for 2 minutes; drain well
• Mix 2 tbs. oil with turmeric, fish sauce, pepper, and salt
• Mix vermicelli with turmeric mixture
• Peel shrimp; make a shallow cut along the back of each
• Cut meat into thin slices
• Wash and cut cabbage into thin slices
• Wash and cut scallion into large pieces
• Peel and slice garlic and onion
• Wash and slice bell pepper
• Heat 2 tbs. oil in a wok or frying pan
• Stir-fry garlic 1 minute
• Add meat, onion, bell pepper and shrimp; stir-fry 2 minutes
• Add vermicelli, scallion, cabbage and bean sprouts; stir-fry 3 minutes

Serving
Serves 4

Crispy Rice Noodles
Bihun Goreng

Ingredients
½ lb. dried Chinese rice vermicelli
¼ lb. bean sprouts
¼ lb. shrimp
¼ lb. beef
1½ cups vegetable oil
½ cup water
¼ green bell pepper
¼ red bell pepper
2 cloves garlic
1 scallion
½ tbs. cornstarch
3 tbs. soy sauce
½ tbs. sugar
¼ tsp. ground pepper
2 tsp. sesame oil

Preparation
• Deep-fry vermicelli over high heat (oil has to be very hot) until puffed (This takes only 5 seconds)
• Place fried vermicelli on a plate; press gently with fingers to break into big pieces
• Cut beef into thin slices
• Mix beef with soy sauce and cornstarch
• Slice ham
• Wash and cut bell peppers into slices
• Wash and cut scallion into large pieces
• Peel shrimp; make a shallow cut along the back of each
• Peel and slice garlic
• Heat 1 tbs. oil
• Stir-fry garlic 1 minute
• Add beef, ham, bell peppers, shrimp, soy sauce, sesame oil, sugar, and pepper
• Stir-fry 3 minutes
• Add water, scallion and bean sprouts; stir-fry 30 seconds

Serving
• Pour hot vegetable-meat sauce over a bed of fried vermicelli shortly before serving
• Serves 2

Fried Noodles
Mi Goreng

Ingredients

1 lb. fresh Chinese wheat or wheat-egg noodles	2 scallions
½ lb. meat (pork, chicken or beef)	2 tbs. fried shallots
½ lb. bean sprouts	3 tbs. vegetable oil
4 cups water	½ tbs. sesame oil
2 cloves garlic	3 tbs. fish sauce
2 celery stalks	3 tbs. soy sauce
	½ tsp. ground pepper

Preparation

- Cut meat into thin slices
- Wash scallion and celery; cut into slices
- Peel and slice garlic
- Bring water in a big pot to a boil
- Add noodles; cook 1-2 minutes until just tender but firm to the bite; stir gently with a fork to separate noodles
- Drain noodles; rinse well with tap water
- Mix noodles with 1 tbs. oil, fish sauce, soy sauce, sesame oil, and pepper
- Heat 2 tbs. oil in a wok or large nonstick pan; stir-fry garlic 1 minute
- Add meat; stir-fry 1 minute
- Add noodles and celery; stir-fry 4-5 minutes over medium heat
- Add bean sprouts and scallions; stir-fry 30 seconds

Serving

- Sprinkle with fried shallots before serving
- Serves 4

Did you know?

- There are many Indonesian dishes that were inspired, a few centuries ago, by dishes from other countries. *Mi goreng* (fried noodles), *lumpia* (springroll) and *pangsit* (wonton), among others, owe their ancestry to Chinese food. However, these dishes have been modified to Indonesian taste and integrated into Indonesian cuisine. In fact, these dishes are as popular in Indonesia as hot dogs or hamburgers in the United States. Street vendors selling these specialties can be found everywhere. Noodles are often served at birthday celebrations as they symbolize long life and good fortune.

Crispy Noodles
Ifu Mi

Ingredients

Sauce

¼ lb. pork (or chicken or beef)
¼ lb. shrimp
1 cup water (or broth)
¹/8 lb. bamboo shoots (from can)
¼ lb. cauliflower
¹/8 lb. snow peas
5 mushrooms
1 carrot
1 clove garlic
2 tbs. vegetable oil
2 tbs. cornstarch
2 tbs. soy sauce

Noodles

¹/3 lb. thin Chinese wheat or wheat-egg noodles
5 cups water
5 tbs. vegetable oil

Preparation

Noodles

- Bring water to a boil
- Add noodles; cook 2 minutes; stir with a fork to separate noodles
- Drain noodles; wash with tap water; drain well; divide into 3 portions
- Heat 2 tbs. oil in a wok or nonstick frying pan
- Spread 1 portion of noodles on the wok or pan; fry 3 minutes
- Turn noodles over, splash in 2 tbs. oil around the edge of the pan; fry 3 minutes
- Repeat for the remaining noodles

Sauce

- Cut pork into thin slices; mix with soy sauce and cornstarch
- Peel garlic and carrot; slice thinly
- Peel shrimp, leaving tails intact
- Wash and cut cauliflower into serving pieces
- Wash snowpeas; remove ends
- Wash mushrooms; cut into slices
- Heat oil in a wok or pot
- Stir-fry garlic 1 minute
- Add meat, shrimp and all vegetables; stir-fry 2 minutes
- Add water (or broth)
- Bring to a short boil

Serving

- Pour hot vegetable-meat sauce over fried noodles shortly before serving
- Serves 2

Seafood

Fried Fish in Sweet and Sour Sauce
Fried Fish Cutlets in Curry Sauce
Fried Fish in Red Coconut Sauce
Fried Fish in Soy Sauce
Fried Fish Rolls in Sweet and Sour Sauce
Egg Fu-Yong
Stir-Fried Shrimp with Ginger
Fried Shrimp and Calamari with Five-Spices
Sautéed Clams in Soy Sauce
Spicy Scallops
Sweet and Sour Shrimp with Fried Potatoes
Stir-Fried Shrimp with Tomato and Bell Pepper
Fried Prawn with Tomato Sauce
Sautéed Prawns
Calamari and Baby Corn in Oyster Sauce
Scallop in Oyster Sauce

Fried Fish in Sweet and Sour Sauce
Ikan Goreng Asam Manis

Ingredients

Fish
1   lb. fish (red snapper can be used)
1   tbs. cooking wine
1   tbs. cornstarch
½   tsp. salt
1½ cups vegetable oil

Sauce
½   cup water
1   piece (½ inch) fresh ginger
1   tbs. cornstarch
1   tbs. ketchup
1¼ tbs. sugar
½   tsp. ground red chilies *(sambal)*, adjust
      amount to taste
½   tsp. white vinegar
½   tsp. fried garlic
¼   tsp. salt

Preparation

Fish
• Scale and clean fish, remove innards
  (fish stores will clean fish)
• Make 3 deep incisions on each side
• Rub fish with wine and salt; refrigerate
  10 minutes
• Heat oil in a wok or nonstick pan
• Coat fish with cornstarch; deep-fry 3
  minutes each side or until crispy

Sauce
• Peel and slice ginger
• Mix cornstarch with 1 tbs. water
• Add ginger to water in a small pot
• Cover pot; simmer 3 minutes
• Remove ginger; add the remaining
  ingredients
• Stir in cornstarch solution
• Bring sauce to a short boil

Serving
• Pour hot sauce over warm fish
• Serve with rice for 2

Tips
• Deep-frying uses a significant amount of hot oil and therefore requires some precautions
  to assure safety. When the food to be fried is wet, it is best to pat it dry with a piece of
  paper towel before placing it gently into the hot oil since the introduction of water to hot
  oil will cause spattering that may burn the skin.
• While frying in the vicinity of boiling or steaming food, it is best to place the pot apart
  from the frying pan to prevent water from splashing into the hot oil.
• When draining paper is placed on a plate to absorb the oil from fried food be sure to place
  the plate and paper far enough away so the paper will not catch fire.
• Also be careful with brandy and other alcohol in the presence of fire or hot surfaces as
  they may promote fire.

Fried Fish Cutlets in Curry Sauce
Ikan Pindang Tumis

Ingredients
1½ lbs. fish cutlets
½   cup water
1   tbs. cooking wine
1   tbs. fried shallots
3   tbs. lime juice
½   tsp. ground red chilies *(sambal)*, adjust amount to taste
¼   tsp. ground turmeric
½   tsp. ground galangal
½   tsp. shrimp paste
1   tsp. fried garlic
1   tbs. sugar
1   tsp. salt
1½ cups vegetable oil

Preparation
• Rub fish with wine; refrigerate 10 minutes
• Heat oil in a wok or nonstick pan
• Pat fish dry with a piece of paper towel
• Deep-fry 8 minutes each side
• Arrange fried fish pieces in a heatproof container
• Prepare sauce by mixing all other ingredients in a small pot
• Bring sauce to a short boil
• Pour sauce over fish (cover fish completely with sauce)
• Cover container; refrigerate 1 hour or overnight
• Heat fish before serving (in a microwave or oven)

Serving
Serve warm with rice for 2

Tip to prevent fish odor in the refrigerator
Fish odor may develop in the refrigerator when fish is stored there. Placing an open container filled with baking soda or ground coffee beans in the refrigerator can prevent the odor development or odor transfer to other foods.

Fried Fish in Red Coconut Sauce
Ikan Bumbu Rujak

Ingredients
1½ lbs. fish cutlets
½   red bell pepper (¼ lb.)
1½ cups vegetable oil
½   cup coconut milk (shake can)
¼   cup water
1   tbs. ground red chilies *(sambal)*, adjust amount to taste
½   tbs. fried shallots
1   tbs. brown sugar
¼   tsp. ground coriander
½   tsp. shrimp paste
1   tsp. fried garlic
½   tsp. salt

Preparation
• Heat oil in a wok or nonstick pan
• Pat fish dry with a piece of paper towel
• Deep-fry 8 minutes each side; set aside
• Grind bell pepper
• Prepare sauce by mixing all ingredients (except fish and oil) in a pot; bring to a boil
• Add fried fish (cover fish completely with sauce)
• Cover pot; simmer 10-15 minutes

Serving
Serve warm with rice for 2

Tip
The red appearance in the original recipe comes from ground red chilies, which are used quite generously. The chilies are important not only to add bulk to the sauce, but also to provide the appetizing aroma and red color. The number of seeds left in the chilies can control the hotness of the dish. The more seeds the hotter the sauce. To reduce the hotness even more without sacrificing too much of the aroma and red color, red bell peppers can be substituted for some of the chilies. The proportion of the chilies to bell peppers can be adjusted to achieve the desirable hotness.

Fried Fish in Soy Sauce
Ikan Goreng Saus Kecap

Ingredients

Fish

1   lb. fish
1   tbs. cooking wine
½   tsp. salt
1½ cups vegetable oil

Sauce

1   piece (¼ inch) fresh ginger
1   chili (red or green)
2   cloves garlic
2   scallions
2   tbs. vegetable oil
1½ tbs. white vinegar
4   tbs. soy sauce
3   tbs. water

Preparation

Fish

• Scale and clean fish, remove innards (fish stores will clean fish)
• Make 3 deep incisions on each side
• Rub fish with wine and salt; refrigerate 20 minutes
• Heat oil in a wok or nonstick pan
• Pat fish dry with a piece of paper towel; deep-fry 3½ minutes each side until crispy

Sauce

• Peel and chop garlic and ginger
• Wash and chop scallions and chili
• Heat oil in a small pot
• Stir-fry garlic and ginger 1 minute
• Add scallions and chili
• Stir-fry for additional 30 seconds
• Add soy sauce, water, and vinegar
• Bring sauce to a short boil

Serving

• Pour hot sauce over warm fish
• Serve with rice for 2

Tip to select fish

The eyes should be crystal clear and the gills should be rosy in color. As a fish loses its freshness, the eyes turn dull and the flesh becomes so soft that an impression remains if it is pressed with the tip of a finger.

Fried Fish Rolls in Sweet and Sour Sauce
Ikan Bungkus Asam Manis

Ingredients

Fish

1	lb. fish fillet (Scrod fillet can be used)
1	egg
7	tbs. cornstarch
6	tbs. water
¼	tsp. ground pepper
½	tsp. salt
1½	cups vegetable oil

Sauce

1½	cups water
1	piece (½ inch) fresh ginger
3	tbs. ketchup
1½	tbs. sugar
½	tsp. ground red chilies (*sambal*), adjust amount to taste
1½	tsp. cornstarch
1½	tsp. vinegar
½	tsp. salt

Preparation

Fish

- Cut fish fillet into thin square slices
- Prepare batter by mixing all other ingredients, except oil
- Heat oil in a wok or frying pan
- Dip fish pieces into batter
- Scoop up fish pieces with a spoon; slide into the oil
- Deep-fry 2 minutes or until golden brown

Sauce

- Peel and slice ginger
- Mix cornstarch with 1 tbs. water
- Mix sugar and 3 tbs. water in a small pot; simmer until solution turns light brown
- Add ginger and the remaining water; bring to a short boil
- Stir in cornstarch solution
- Add all other ingredients; cook 30 seconds

Serving

- Pour hot sauce over warm fried fish
- Serve with rice for 2

Stir-Fried Shrimp with Ginger
Udang Tumis Jahe

Ingredients

½	lb. shrimp		1	scallion
1	piece (1 inch) fresh ginger		1	tbs. cooking wine
1	stalk parsley leaves		2	tbs. vegetable oil
1	clove garlic		1	tbs. soy sauce

Preparation
- Peel shrimp, leaving tails intact; make a shallow cut along the back of each
- Chop parsley leaves
- Peel and finely grate ginger
- Wash and chop scallion
- Peel and slice garlic
- Heat oil in a wok or frying pan
- Stir-fry garlic and ginger 1 minute
- Add shrimp, scallion, parsley, soy sauce, and wine
- Stir-fry 3-5 minutes (depending on shrimp size) or until shrimp turns pink

Serving
Serve with rice for 2

Egg Fu-Yong
Telur Fu-yong

Ingredients

Omelet

4	eggs
1	medium onion
1	carrot
¼	leek
¼	lb. crab meat
1	tbs. vegetable oil
2	tbs. sliced ham
¼	tsp. ground pepper
1	tsp. garlic powder
1½	tsp. salt

Sauce

½	cup water
1	piece (½ inch) fresh ginger
½	carrot
2	tbs. fresh or frozen green peas
1	tbs. ketchup
1	tbs. sugar
1	tsp. ground red chilies *(sambal)*, adjust amount to taste
1	tsp. fried garlic
1	tsp. cornstarch
2	tsp. vinegar
½	tsp. salt
dash pepper	

Preparation

Omelet

- Peel and shred carrot
- Peel and chop onion
- Tear crabmeat into long pieces
- Slice and wash leek
- Break eggs into a bowl
- Add spices to eggs; beat lightly with a fork
- Add all other ingredients, except oil
- Heat oil in a nonstick pan
- Fry egg mixture over medium heat 2-3 minutes, then flip it like an omelet
- Using spatula, press the omelet lightly so the inside part cooks well
- Continue frying until the egg mixture is completely cooked

Sauce

- Peel carrot and julienne into 5 inch pieces
- Peel and slice ginger
- Mix cornstarch with 1 tbs. water
- Mix sugar with 2 tbs. water in a small pot
- Heat sugar solution until brownish, but do not burn
- Add the remaining water carefully
- Add all other ingredients, except green peas and cornstarch solution
- Simmer 4 minutes
- Stir in cornstarch solution
- Add green peas; cook 1 minute

Serving
- Pour sauce over warm omelet shortly before serving for 2

Fried Shrimp and Calamari with Five-Spices
Udang dan Cumi-cumi Goreng Rempah

Ingredients

½ lb. calamari
¼ lb. shrimp
1½ cups vegetable oil
4 leaves lettuce
4 cloves garlic

2 scallions
8 tbs. cornstarch
½ tsp. five-spice powder
1 tsp. salt

Preparation

- Peel and chop garlic
- Wash and chop scallions
- Wash lettuce; drain well
- Slice lettuce; spread over 2 plates

Shrimp

- Peel shrimp, leaving tails intact; make a shallow cut along the back of each
- Coat shrimp with cornstarch
- Heat oil in a wok or frying pan
- Deep-fry shrimp 1-2 minutes until crispy; set aside
- Heat 1 tbs. oil in a wok or pan
- Stir-fry half of the chopped garlic 1 minute
- Add fried shrimp, half of the chopped scallions, dash of five-spice powder and salt
- Stir-fry 1 minute
- Pour shrimp over a bed of sliced lettuce

Calamari

- Peel calamari, remove the inside part and head (cleaned calamari are available in some stores); cut into rings of 1 inch wide
- Cover calamari pieces with cornstarch
- Heat oil in a wok or frying pan
- Deep-fry calamari pieces 3 minutes until crispy; set aside
- Heat 1 tbs. oil in a wok or pan
- Stir-fry the remaining chopped garlic 1 minute
- Add fried calamari, the remaining chopped scallions, dash of five-spice powder and salt
- Stir-fry 1 minute
- Pour calamari over a bed of sliced lettuce

Serving

Serve with rice for 2

Sautéed Clams in Soy Sauce
Sambal Goreng Kerang

Ingredients

1¼ lbs. (12-16 pieces) clams
1   piece (1 inch) fresh ginger
1   green or red chilies
2   cloves garlic
½   onion

½   cup water
2   tbs. vegetable oil
2   tbs. soy sauce
1   tbs. sugar
½   tsp. cornstarch

Preparation

Cleaning of clams

• Wash and brush the outside shell of clams

• Soak clams in 4 cups of water 10 minutes

Cooking

• Peel and slice ginger, onion and garlic

• Wash and slice chilies

• Mix cornstarch with 1 tbs. water

• Heat oil in a wok or pot

• Stir-fry ginger and garlic 1 minute

• Add onion and chili; stir-fry 2 minutes

• Add soy sauce, sugar, cornstarch solution, and water

• Bring to a boil, stirring occasionally

• Add clams

• Cover wok or pot; simmer 5 minutes until the shells open

Serving

Serve with rice for 2

Spicy Scallops
Kerang Kepah Pedas

Ingredients

Scallop

½   lb. scallops
1   piece (¼ inch) fresh ginger
1   egg white
1   scallion
1   tbs. cooking wine
3   tbs. cornstarch
½   cup vegetable oil
dash salt

Sauce

1   piece (¼ inch) fresh ginger
½   tbs. ketchup
5   tbs. water
½   tsp. ground red chilies *(sambal)*, adjust
     amount to taste
1   tsp. white vinegar
½   tsp. fried garlic
¼   tsp. cornstarch
¾   tsp. sugar
dash salt

Preparation

Scallops

• Wash scallion; cut into big pieces

• Peel and slice ginger

• Crush scallion and ginger pieces

• Marinate scallops with wine, scallion, ginger and salt for 15 minutes

• Dip scallops into egg white, then cornstarch until entirely coated

• Heat oil in a wok or nonstick frying pan

• Deep-fry scallops 2 minutes each side over medium heat; set aside

Sauce

• Peel and slice ginger

• Mix all ingredients in a small pot

• Bring sauce to a short boil

• Remove ginger before serving

Serving

• Pour sauce over warm scallops shortly before serving

• Serve as an appetizer or with rice as a main dish for 2

Fried Prawns with Tomato Sauce
Udang Goreng Saus Tomat

Ingredients
1   lb. prawns
1   egg white
1   tbs. cooking wine
5   tbs. cornstarch (or bread crumbs)
¼   tsp. baking soda
2   tsp. salt
½   cup vegetable oil
Ketchup (for dipping)

Preparation
• Peel prawns, leaving tails intact
• Prepare batter by mixing all ingredients (except oil, prawns, and ketchup)
• Heat oil in a wok or frying pan
• Dip prawns into the batter and slide into the hot oil
• Deep-fry prawns until golden brown

Serving
Serve fried prawns with ketchup dip as an appetizer or with rice as a main dish

Stir-Fried Shrimp with Tomato and Bell Pepper
Udang Tumis Tomat dan Paprika

Ingredients

1	lb. shrimp		1	scallion
1	medium size tomato		2	tbs. vegetable oil
1	red bell pepper		1	tbs. oyster sauce
2	cloves garlic		3	tbs. soy sauce
1	small onion		1	tsp. sugar

Preparation

- Peel and slice garlic
- Peel onion and cut into 4 equal wedges; separate layers
- Wash and cut bell pepper and scallion into pieces
- Cut tomato into 8 equal wedges
- Heat oil in a wok or frying pan
- Stir-fry garlic and bell pepper 2 minutes
- Add onion and shrimp; stir-fry 2 minutes
- Add tomato and all other ingredients; stir-fry 1 minute

Serving

Serve with rice for 2

Did you know?

Short exposure to high heat is the key to stir-frying vegetables for color appeal and crispness. Stir-fried dishes are their best when served immediately. Stir-frying preserves color, texture, and taste as well as nutritional value.

Sweet and Sour Shrimp with Fried Potatoes
Selada Udang

Ingredients:

Shrimp
½ lb. shrimp
8   leaves lettuce
2   shallots
¼   cup water
1   tbs. white vinegar
1   tbs. margarine
1   tbs. soy sauce
½   tbs. sugar
½   tsp. salt

Fried potatoes
3   potatoes
1½ cups vegetable oil

Preparation

Shrimp
• Peel shrimp, leaving tail intact
• Peel and slice shallots
• Heat margarine in a pot
• Stir-fry shallots 2 minutes
• Add shrimp; stir-fry 1 minute
• Add soy sauce, vinegar, salt, sugar, and water
• Bring to a short boil

Fried potatoes
• Cut potatoes into serving pieces
• Heat oil in a wok or frying-pot
• Deep-fry potatoes 2½ minutes; set aside
• Reheat oil
• Deep-fry potatoes for an additional 4 minutes

Serving
• Wash lettuce and cut into large pieces
• Place fried potatoes and lettuce on a plate
• Pour shrimp over fried potatoes and lettuce
• Serves 2

Did you know?
Potatoes appear to have been first cultivated between 4000 and 7000 years ago in the Andes Mountains of Bolivia and Peru. The potato was a major food of the Indians living at high altitudes in the Andes, because few other crops could be grown under such conditions. In the 16th century the Spanish explorers brought potatoes to Spain, then introduced them to Europe. Potatoes contain protein, phosphorus, iron, and vitamin C.

Sautéed Prawns
Udang Tumis

Ingredients
½   lb. prawn
1   egg
2   tbs. vegetable oil
1   tbs. cornstarch
1   tsp. garlic powder
¼   tsp. salt
dash pepper
Parsley

Preparation
- Using a sharp knife make a cut along the back of each shrimp; remove vein
- Spread open the inside surface of the shrimp; score to prevent it from curling during frying
- Mix all ingredients (except prawn, oil, and parsley)
- Spread mixture on the inside surface of shrimp; sprinkle with finely chopped parsley
- Heat oil in a nonstick pan
- Fry shrimp 1 minute each side

Serving
- Serve as an appetizer or with rice as a main dish
- Serves 2

Calamari and Baby Corn in Oyster Sauce
Cumi-cumi Saus Tiram

Ingredients

¼ lb. baby corn
½ lb. calamari
1 piece (1 inch) fresh ginger
1 chili (red or green)
2 cloves garlic
½ small onion
2 tbs. vegetable oil

½ tbs. cooking wine
1 tbs. oyster sauce
1 tbs. soy sauce
2 tbs. water
1 tsp. cornstarch
1 tsp. sugar

Preparation

• Clean calamari; remove the skin and head (cleaned calamari is available in some stores)
• Cut calamari into 1½ x ¾ inch pieces; score crosswise and lengthwise
• Peel and slice garlic
• Peel and cut onion into 4 equal wedges; separate layers
• Peel and finely grate ginger
• Wash and chop chili
• Slice baby corn into half
• Mix cornstarch with water
• Heat oil in a wok or frying pan
• Stir-fry garlic 1 minute
• Add ginger, onion and chili; stir-fry 30 seconds
• Add calamari; stir-fry 1 minute
• Add wine, soy sauce, oyster sauce, sugar and cornstarch solution; stir-fry 1 minute

Serving
Serve with rice for 2

Tip
It is important to avoid cooking calamari too long. When overcooked, calamari loses its tenderness and becomes tough or chewy.

Scallops in Oyster Sauce
Kerang Kepah Saus Tiram

Ingredients
¾ lb. scallops
1   piece (½ inch) fresh ginger
½   green bell pepper
½   red bell pepper
2   cloves garlic
1   small onion

2   tbs. vegetable oil
1   tbs. cooking wine
2   tbs. oyster sauce
1   tbs. soy sauce
1   tsp. sugar

Preparation
• Peel and cut onion into quarters; separate layers
• Cut bell peppers into ¾ x ¾ inch squares
• Peel garlic and ginger; cut into slices
• Marinate scallops with ginger, wine, oyster sauce and soy sauce
• Heat oil in a wok or frying pan
• Stir-fry garlic 1 minute
• Add bell peppers and onion; stir-fry 3 minutes
• Add scallops and sugar
• Stir-fry 2-4 minutes, depending on scallop size (slice scallops into half if scallops are large)

Serving
Serve with rice for 2

Poultry

Barbecue Chicken
Chicken in Red Coconut Sauce
Chicken in Soy Sauce
Chicken Liver with Shrimp and Coconut
Chicken on Skewers with Peanut Dressing
Chicken Pot Pie
Chicken Salad
Chicken with Bean Sprouts
Crispy Curry Fried Chicken
Crispy Fried Chicken with Five-Spices
Curry Chicken
Fried Chicken with Worcestershire Sauce
Steamed Ginger Chicken
Stir-Fried Chicken in Broth
Crispy Duck
Duck with Lime Sauce

Chicken on Skewers with Peanut Dressing
Sate Ayam

Ingredients

Meat

1   lb. boned, skinned chicken, preferably thigh
1   tbs. vegetable oil
3   tbs. soy sauce
1   tbs. sugar
1   tsp. garlic powder
20 bamboo skewers
dash coriander

Sauce

½   tbs. ground red chilies *(sambal)*, adjust amount to taste
4   tbs. chunky peanut butter
1   tbs. fried shallots
½   tsp. garlic powder
1   tsp. brown sugar
¾   tsp. salt
½   cup water

Preparation

Meat

- Cut chicken into 1 x ¾ x ½ inch pieces
- Mix chicken with soy sauce, sugar, garlic and coriander; refrigerate 1 hour or overnight
- Thread 5 pieces of meat onto each skewer. The meat should be arranged on the skewer so the cubes run lengthwise.

Sauce

- Mix all ingredients for sauce in a small pot
- Bring sauce to a short boil, stirring occasionally to prevent burning

Cooking meat on charcoal grill (for the best result)

- Grill meat 3-4 minutes each side until meat is cooked

Cooking meat in oven (alternative)

- Preheat oven to the highest setting
- Put meat on a double layer of aluminum foil brushed with oil
- In a gas oven place meat on the floor of oven (not on rack). In an electric oven place meat on a rack closest to the heat source. Keep the skewers away from the heat to prevent burning. Leave oven door ajar to allow skewers to project outward.
- Cook 4-5 minutes each side until meat is cooked.

Serving

- Pour sauce over meat before serving
- Serve with rice
- Makes 24 skewers

Fried Chicken with Worcestershire Sauce
Ayam Goreng Saus Inggris

Ingredients

Chicken & marinade

2   chicken legs (1½ lbs.)
1   piece (1 inch) fresh ginger
2   tbs. cooking wine
2   tbs. soy sauce
2   cups vegetable oil

Sauce

¼   scallion
3   tbs. Worcestershire sauce
1   tbs. cooking wine
3   tbs. soy sauce
3   tbs. water
1½ tbs. sugar
¼   tsp. ground pepper
1   tsp. fried garlic
1½ tsp. sesame oil
1   tsp. margarine

Preparation

Chicken & marinade

- Cut chicken into serving pieces
- Peel and slice ginger
- Marinate chicken pieces with ginger, wine, and soy sauce for 1 hour
- Heat oil in a wok or frying pan
- Deep-fry chicken pieces over medium heat 6 minutes each side

Sauce

- Crush fried garlic
- Wash and chop scallion
- Melt margarine
- Mix all ingredients in a small bowl

Serving

Serve fried chicken with sauce and rice for 2

Did you know?

When added in small amounts, sugar can enhance and balance food flavors.

Steamed Ginger Chicken
Ayam Jahe Kukus

Ingredients
½   chicken (1½ lbs.)
1   piece (1 inch) fresh ginger
2   scallions
4   tbs. cooking wine
1   tsp. fried garlic
1   tsp. salt
dash pepper

Preparation
• Cut chicken into serving pieces
• Wash and finely slice 1 scallion; set aside for garnish
• Cut the other scallion into 4 pieces
• Peel and slice ginger
• Crush scallion and ginger lightly
• Mix all ingredients
• Marinate chicken pieces with the mixture in a heatproof bowl for 30 minutes
• Steam marinated chicken in the heatproof bowl for 30 minutes

Serving
• Sprinkle chicken pieces with fine slices of scallion
• Serve with rice for 2

Tips
Poultry is perishable; therefore, it should be stored and prepared properly.
• Store properly wrapped poultry in the refrigerator only for 1 to 2 days. For longer storage, keep poultry in the freezer. When freezing any food, divide into portions that will be needed so that it is not necessary to thaw the whole piece in order to use only a portion of it.
• Wash poultry before preparing it for cooking
• Wash hands after preparing poultry and before touching other materials
• Cook poultry completely at one time. Never partially cook, then store and finish cooking at a later date.
• Store leftover cooked poultry or broth as quickly as possible in the refrigerator. Cover and use within 1 to 2 days or freeze for longer storage.

Chicken Pot Pie
Pastel Tutup

Ingredients
Filling

1   lb. chicken with bones (or ¾ lb. boneless)
½   lb. carrots
2   oz. cellophane noodles
2   stalks parsley
2   cups water
1   cup milk
1½ cups frozen green peas
½   tbs. fried shallots
½   tsp. ground nutmeg
1   tsp. fried garlic
2   tsp. cornstarch
½   tsp. sugar
2¼ tsp. salt
dash pepper

Potato mix

1   egg
1½ lbs. potatoes
2   tbs. margarine
3   tbs. dried milk
½   tsp. salt
dash nutmeg
dash pepper

Preparation
Filling

- Boil water; cook chicken 10 minutes
- Cut chicken into small pieces
- Cut peeled carrots into small squares
- Wash and chop parsley
- Soak cellophane noodles in hot water for 30 seconds; cut into 3 inch pieces
- Mix cornstarch with 1 tbs. water
- Bring broth to a boil
- Add all ingredients; cook 2 minutes

Potato mix

- Wash potatoes; steam until soft
- Peel potatoes and mash while warm
- Add all other ingredients and mix

Finishing

- Fill a heat-proof container with filling until about 1 inch to the top
- Spread ½ inch thick potato mix on a sheet of aluminum foil slightly larger than the container's rim
- Flip the sheet on the container with the potato facing the filling
- Press sheet on the container rim
- Remove sheet and remnants of potato
- Bake 20 minutes at 400ºF

Serving
Serve warm as a snack, appetizer or main dish

Barbecue Chicken
Ayam Panggang

Ingredients
½   chicken (1½ lbs.)
1   clove garlic
1   tbs. ground red chilies *(sambal)*, adjust amount to taste
2   tbs. brown sugar
½   tbs. margarine
2   tbs. soy sauce
2   tbs. lime juice
dash pepper

Preparation
- Peel and mince garlic
- Melt margarine
- Prepare seasoning sauce by mixing all ingredients (except chicken) in a small bowl
- Cut chicken into serving pieces or leave whole
- Broil chicken 7 minutes each side
- Baste grilled chicken with sauce
- Broil chicken 10-15 minutes each side, basting second side with sauce before continuing to broil

Serving
Serve with rice for 2

Crispy Fried Chicken with Five-Spices
Ayam Goreng Rempah

Ingredients
½   chicken (1½ lbs.)
4   tbs. cornstarch
1   tsp. five-spice powder
2   tsp. garlic powder
2   tsp. salt
2   cups vegetable oil

Preparation
• Cut chicken into serving pieces
• Mix all dry ingredients
• Coat chicken pieces with mixture
• Deep-fry chicken pieces over medium heat 6-8 minutes each side until crispy and golden brown

Serving
Serve with rice and chili sauce for 2

Stir-Fried Chicken with Broth
Ayam Bakmoi

Ingredients

Meat

1½ lbs. chicken with bones
1   large piece beancurd (tofu)
2   cloves garlic
½   stalk celery
1   onion
4   tbs. soy sauce
¼   tsp. ground pepper
1   tsp. sesame oil
1   cup vegetable oil

Soup

4   cups water
1   tsp. fried garlic
3   tsp. salt
dash pepper

Preparation

Meat

- Cut beancurd into 1x½x½ inch pieces
- Heat oil in a wok or nonstick pan
- Deep-fry beancurd 5 minutes; set aside
- Peel and slice garlic and onion
- Cut celery into slices
- Cut chicken meat into small pieces
- Set aside chicken bones for soup
- Heat 2 tbs. oil in a wok or pan
- Stir-fry garlic 1 minute
- Add onion; stir-fry 1-2 minutes

- Add chicken, fried beancurd, celery, pepper, soy sauce and sesame oil
- Stir-fry 6 minutes

Soup

- Bring water to a boil in a pot
- Add chicken bones, salt, pepper and fried garlic
- Cover pot; simmer 10 minutes
- Remove chicken bones

Serving

Serve with rice for 2

Tip to prevent eye irritation from onion

The annoyance of chopping onions due to the eye-irritating substance in onions can be avoided by putting the onions in a freezer for 20 minutes prior to chopping them. The substance is released as a result of the enzyme action brought about by rupturing the onion cells. Freezing inactivates the enzyme.

Chicken in Soy Sauce
Ayam Semur

Ingredients
3   chicken legs (2 lbs.)
1¼ cups water
½   tbs. vegetable oil
1   tbs. white vinegar
1½ tbs. fried shallots
6   tbs. soy sauce
1½ tbs. sugar
½   tsp. ground galangal
½   tsp. ground nutmeg
¼   tsp. ground pepper
1   tsp. fried garlic

Preparation
• Cut chicken into serving pieces
• Brush roasting pan with vegetable oil
• Broil chicken pieces 15 minutes each side
• Bring water in a pot to boil
• Add chicken and all other ingredients
• Cover pot; simmer 12-15 minutes

Serving
Serve with rice for 3

Did you know?
• Soy sauce originated in China some 2,500 years ago and was introduced in Japan in the 7th century by Buddhist priests. In Japan, about equal amounts of soybeans and wheat are used in making soy sauce. In China, more soybeans and less wheat are used.
• Good soy sauce contains large amounts of amino acids, especially glutamic acids. Amino acids are the building blocks of proteins.

Chicken with Bean Sprouts
Ayam Tauge

Ingredients

½ lb. boneless chicken	1½ tbs. soy sauce
¼ lb. bean sprout	1 tsp. sesame oil
1 small onion	½ tsp. sugar
1 scallion	1 tsp. salt
1 tbs. cornstarch	1 cup vegetable oil

Preparation
• Peel and slice onion
• Wash and cut scallion into big pieces
• Cut chicken into pieces
• Mix chicken pieces with soy sauce and cornstarch
• Heat oil in a wok or frying pan
• Deep-fry chicken pieces 3 minutes; set aside
• Heat 1 tbs. oil in a wok or frying pan
• Add onion; stir-fry 1 minute
• Add fried chicken pieces, scallion, bean sprouts, sugar, salt and sesame oil
• Stir-fry 30 seconds

Serving
Serve with rice for 2

Did you know?
• Bean sprouts are made by soaking soy beans with a large quantity of water. The water is drained when the skin splits the next day, leaving the beans covered in a wet folded linen. The bean and linen should be maintained moist the whole time. It takes 2-3 days for the sprouts to fully grow. Bean sprouts are rich in vitamin C. On a moisture-free basis, bean sprouts contain about 50% proteins.

• Short exposure to high heat is the key to stir-frying vegetables for color appeal and crispness. Stir-fried dishes are their best when served immediately. Stir-frying preserves color, texture and taste as well as nutritional value.

Chicken in Red Coconut Sauce
Ayam Panike

Ingredients
3   chicken legs
1   piece (¼ inch) fresh ginger
¹/8 red bell pepper
½   cup coconut milk (shake can)
½   cup water
2   candlenuts
2   cloves garlic
2   shallots
½   tbs. vegetable oil
1   tsp. ground red chilies *(sambal)*, adjust amount to taste
½   tsp. ground lemongrass
½   tsp. ground galangal
½   tsp. shrimp paste
1   tsp. lime juice
1½ tsp. sugar
½   tsp. salt

Preparation
• Cut chicken into serving pieces
• Brush roasting pan with vegetable oil
• Broil chicken pieces 15 minutes each side
• Peel and slice ginger
• Peel shallots and garlic
• Grind shallots, garlic, bell pepper and candlenuts in a food processor (add 3 tbs. water to facilitate grinding)
• Mix all ingredients (except chicken) in a pot; bring to a boil
• Add chicken
• Cover pot; simmer 20 minutes, stirring occasionally

Serving
Serve with rice for 2

Chicken Liver with Shrimp and Coconut
Sambal Goreng Hati

Ingredients
1   lb. chicken livers
¼   lb. shrimp
¼   cup coconut milk (shake can)
3   cups water
1   medium size tomato
1   tbs. fried shallots
1   tsp. ground red chilies *(sambal)*, adjust amount to taste
¼   tsp. ground lemongrass
1   tsp. ground galangal
½   tsp. shrimp paste
2   tsp. fried garlic
1   tsp. sugar
1   tsp. salt

Preparation
• Bring 2 cups of water to a boil
• Add chicken liver; cook 5 minutes
• Remove liver; discard broth
• Cut liver into big pieces
• Peel shrimp, leaving the tail intact
• Cut tomato into 8 equal wedges
• Bring 1 cup of water in a pot to a boil
• Add all ingredients
• Cover pot; simmer 5 minutes

Serving
Serve with rice for 2

Did you know?
Chicken liver is a rich source of vitamins, especially vitamin B12.

Crispy Curry Fried Chicken
Ayam Goreng Kunir

Ingredients
2   chicken legs (or any other parts)
2   cloves garlic
1   tbs. water
1   tsp. ground turmeric
½   tsp. salt
2   cups vegetable oil
dash pepper

Preparation
- Peel and mince garlic
- Mix all ingredients, except chicken to form paste
- Rub chicken with paste; refrigerate 1 hour or overnight
- Deep-fry over medium heat until crisp and golden brown

Serving
Serve with rice for 2

Memories
    I associate this dish with pleasurable family picnics I had as a child. On Sundays I used to go with my family to a natural pool in the countryside. The place is called *Banyubiru*, which means blue water. My mother always brought a lot of food and snacks. I remember how I disliked carrying all the foods from the car, although I enjoyed eating them. I often told her that we brought too much food, but she just smiled. Indeed, all the food was usually gone at the end of the day. As my mother always said, "Swimming creates an appetite." To my delight, this fried chicken often appeared in the food basket. It is indeed an ideal dish for a picnic because it can be eaten hot or at room temperature. When served at a picnic, it is best to prepare the chicken in rather small pieces.

    We usually spent almost the whole day there, swimming and playing. Clean fresh water was constantly provided by a well at a corner of the pool. At the other side of the pool, the water continuously flowed to a nearby river. I avoided swimming close to the bubbling well because I was afraid it would suck me in. My father tried to convince me that my worry was without merit since the pressure generated by the well would push me out, but this never calmed my anxiety. There were also some fish in the pool, some of them were 2 feet long. I always felt funny when my leg accidentally touched a fish while swimming and I never got used to it even after many years.

Curry Chicken
Ayam Kari

Ingredients
½   chicken (1½ lbs.)
2   lime leaves (or 2 square inches lemon peel)
½   cup coconut milk (shake can)
¾   cup water
½   tbs. vegetable oil
1   tbs. fried shallots
¼   tsp. ground lemongrass
½   tsp. ground coriander
½   tsp. ground turmeric
½   tsp. shrimp paste
1   tsp. fried garlic
½   tsp. sugar
1¼ tsp. salt

Preparation
• Cut chicken into serving pieces
• Brush roasting pan with vegetable oil
• Broil chicken pieces 15 minutes each side
• Mix all ingredients (except chicken) in a pot; bring to a boil
• Add chicken pieces
• Cover pot; simmer 20 minutes, stirring occasionally

Serving
Serve with rice for 2

Scallops in Oyster Sauce

Barbecue Chicken

Chicken Salad

Steamed Ginger Chicken

Duck with Lime Sauce

Beef on Skewers

Beef in Red Coconut Sauce

Spiced Coconut Beef

Pork on Skewers

Fried Pork Chops in Soy Sauce

Fried Ribs

Fried Sausage with Five-Spices

Coconut Pudding

Sweet Yucca Snack

Sweet Coconut Rice Balls

Avocado Fruit Cocktail & Avocado Coffiee Drink

Chicken Salad
Ayam Selada

Ingredients

Salad

¾ lb. chicken with bones or ½ lb. boneless
1 piece (¼ inch) fresh ginger
10 wonton sheets
8 lettuce leaves
¼ cups vegetable oil
3 cups water
2 tbs. roasted sesame seeds
1 tbs. salt

Sauce

2 tbs. vinegar
4 tbs. vegetable oil
1 tbs. soy sauce
1 tbs. sugar
¼ tsp. ground pepper
½ tsp. salt

Preparation

- Prepare sauce by mixing all ingredients for sauce; set aside
- Peel and slice ginger
- Add salt and ginger to water in a pot
- Bring water to a boil
- Add chicken piece by piece so that water continues boiling
- Cover pot; simmer 10 minutes
- Remove chicken and cut into small pieces; set aside
- Cut wonton sheets into ¼ inch slices
- Heat oil and deep-fry wonton sheets 20 seconds; set aside
- Wash and slice lettuce thinly
- Place lettuce on a bowl
- Add chicken and sauce, then mix
- Add fried wonton sheets on top and sprinkle with sesame seeds

Serving

Serve as salad for 2

Did you know?

Archaeological evidence indicates that sesame was cultivated in Palestine and Syria around 3000 BC and in Babylon in 1750 BC. An Egyptian tomb bears a 4,000 year old drawing of a baker adding sesame to bread dough. In 1298 Marco Polo observed the Persians using sesame oil for cooking, body massage, medicinal purposes, illumination, cosmetics, and lubricating primitive machinery.

Duck with Lime Sauce
Bebek Panggang Saus Jeruk Limau

Ingredients

Duck
½ duckling (2 lbs.)
1 tbs. thyme
1 tbs. salt
4 cups water

Sauce
1 tbs. cooking wine
2 tbs. sugar
4 tbs. water
¼ tsp. cornstarch
½ tsp. salt
½ lime
Dash pepper

Preparation

Duck
• Wash duck and remove excess fat
• Rub duck with salt and thyme
• Refrigerate 1 hour or overnight
• Bake 20 minutes at 500°F
• Bring water to a boil; set aside
• Remove duck from the oven and place in a strainer; drain melted fat
• Pour boiling water over duck
• Bake again 45 minutes at 300°F
• Continue baking 10-15 minutes at 500°F or until brown

Sauce
• Press lime to obtain 3 tbs. juice
• Mix cornstarch with 1 tbs. water
• Mix sugar with the remaining water in a small pot
• Heat sugar solution until brownish
• Add all other ingredients
• Mix sauce; bring to a short boil

Serving
• Cut duck into slices
• Serve with rice and sauce for 2

Tip to easily clean grease from oven
Turn the oven off after removing the duck from the oven. Place an open bowl containing 2 tbs. of ammonia in the oven for an hour. Remove bowl from the oven and wipe the entire inside surface of the oven with wet towel. Due to its volatility, ammonia reaches all spots in the oven allowing effortless complete cleaning of the oven. Although ammonia should not be inhaled directly, it is harmless when used as described above. Ammonia is available in supermarket at low price.

Crispy Duck
Bebek Goreng

Ingredients

Duck
½   duckling (2 lbs.)
1   piece (¼ inch) fresh ginger
1   scallion
2   tbs. soy sauce
¾   tsp. five-spice powder
3   cups vegetable oil

Dip
2   tsp. salt
2   tsp. ground pepper

Preparation
• Peel and cut ginger into 3 slices
• Wash scallion; cut into big pieces
• Mix five-spice powder, soy sauce, ginger and scallion
• Wash duck and remove excess fat
• Rub duck with soy sauce mixture; refrigerate 1 hour or overnight
• Steam 2 hours
• Heat oil in a wok or deep frying pan
• Deep-fry over medium heat 4 minutes each side
• Mix salt and pepper for dip

Serving
• Cut duck into slices
• Serve with rice and salt-pepper dip for 2

Tip to cut duck into halves
First remove any excess fat from the duck cavity, and then trim off neck skin. Cut duck through the breastbone with a cleaver. Turn duck over and cut backbone in two.

Beef

Beef on Skewers
Beef in Red Coconut Sauce
Curry Beef
Beef-Potato Patties
Beef Broccoli
Spiced Coconut Beef

Beef on Skewers
Sate Komo

Ingredients

1	lb. beef	½	tsp. ground coriander
1	cup coconut milk (shake can)	½	tsp. ground turmeric
2	lime leaves (or 2 square inches lemon peel)	¼	tsp. ground cumin
		½	tsp. shrimp paste
1	piece (½ inch) fresh ginger	1	tsp. fried garlic
½	tbs. fried shallots	1	tsp. salt
½	tbs. sugar	20	bamboo skewers

Preparation

- Cut beef into cubes of 1x¾x½ inch
- Mix all ingredients (except beef) in a pot; bring to a boil
- Add beef; cover pot; simmer 30 minutes
- Remove cover; simmer until most liquid evaporates, stirring occasionally to prevent burning
- Thread 5 pieces of meat onto each skewer. The meat should be arranged on the skewer so that the cubes run lengthwise.

Cooking meat on charcoal grill (for the best result)
- Grill meat 1 minute each side until brown

Cooking meat in oven (alternative)
- Preheat oven to the highest setting
- Put meat on a double layer of aluminum foil brushed with vegetable oil
- In a gas oven place meat on the floor of oven (not on rack). In an electric oven place meat on a rack closest to the heat source. Keep the skewers away from the heat to prevent burning; leave oven door ajar to allow skewers to project outward.
- Cook 2-3 minutes each side until meat turns brown, but not burning

Serving
- Serve with rice
- Makes 20 skewers

Tips to prevent burning of the bamboo skewers
Soak the skewers in water for several hours before using or wrap the ends in aluminum foil.

Beef in Red Coconut Sauce
Daging Bali

Ingredients
1½ lbs. beef
½   cup coconut milk (shake can)
4   cups water
1   red bell pepper
1   piece (½ inch) fresh ginger
1½ tbs. dark brown sugar
1   tbs. ground red chilies *(sambal)*, adjust amount to taste
2   tbs. fried shallots
½   tbs. fried garlic
½   tsp. shrimp paste
1½ tsp. salt

Preparation
• Cut beef into 2x1½x½ inch pieces
• Bring 2 cups of water in a pot to a boil
• Add beef; cook 5 minutes
• Set aside beef; discard broth
• Peel and slice ginger
• Wash and grind bell pepper
• Mix all ingredients with the remaining water in a pot; bring to a boil
• Cover pot; simmer 45 minutes or until meat is tender

Serving
Serve with rice for 4

Curry Beef
Daging Kari

Ingredients
1½ lbs. beef
½ cup coconut milk (shake can)
4 cups water
2 lime leaves (or 2 square inches lemon peel)
1 piece (½ inch) fresh ginger
1 tbs. fried shallots
½ tbs. fried garlic
½ tsp. ground coriander
½ tsp. ground turmeric
¼ tsp. ground galangal
¼ tsp. ground cumin
½ tsp. shrimp paste
1 tsp. sugar
1½ tsp. salt

Preparation
• Cut beef into 2x1½x½ inch pieces
• Bring 2 cups water in a pot to a boil
• Add beef; cook 5 minutes
• Set aside beef; discard broth
• Peel and slice ginger
• Mix all ingredients with the remaining water in a pot; bring to a boil
• Cover pot; simmer 45 minutes or until meat is tender

Serving
Serve with rice for 4

Did you know?
Beef provides a good source of protein, iron, phosphorus, copper, zinc, vitamin A, and B vitamins (vitamin B12, vitamin B6, biotin, niacin, pantothenic acid, and thiamin). The calories in meat depend mostly upon the amount of fat it contains.

Beef-Potato Patties
Perkedel Daging

Ingredients
½   lb. ground beef
¾   lb. potatoes
1   egg
2   tbs. fried shallots
2   tbs. all-purpose flour
1½ tsp. ground nutmeg
½   tsp. ground pepper
1   tsp. garlic powder
1   tsp. sugar
2   tsp. salt
1½ cups vegetable oil

Preparation
• Steam potatoes until cooked
• Peel potatoes; mash while warm
• Add the remaining ingredients (except oil); mix
• Make a ball of 1 tbs. of the mixture; flatten it to form a disk with diameter of 1¾ inches and thickness of ½ inch; continue with the rest of the mixture
• Heat oil in a wok or frying pan
• Deep-fry 2-3 minutes until light brown

Serving
• Serve as an appetizer or as a main dish with rice and chili sauce
• Makes 40 pieces

Tip
The beef-potato mixture should be firm and dry so that it will not disintegrate during frying.

Did you know?
Steaming preserves flavors and food nutrients through the use of steam temperature rather than destroying them by boiling in higher temperatures and then discarding the nutritious water.

Beef Broccoli
Daging Brokoli

Ingredients
1   lb. broccoli
½   lb. beef
1   piece (½ inch) fresh ginger
½   medium size onion
2   cloves garlic
1   tbs. cooking wine
2   tbs. vegetable oil

1   tbs. oyster sauce
1½ tbs. soy sauce
1   tbs. water
2   tsp. cornstarch
1   tsp. sugar
½   tsp. salt

Preparation
- Mix soy sauce, cornstarch and water
- Cut beef into thin slices; mix with soy sauce mixture
- Peel garlic and ginger; cut into thin slices
- Peel and cut onion into 4 equal wedges; separate layers
- Wash broccoli; remove stem; cut flowerettes into serving size
- Dip broccoli in boiling water for 30 seconds; plunge into cold water and drain
- Heat 1 tbs. oil in a wok or pan
- Stir-fry beef until cooked (20 seconds); set aside
- Heat 1 tbs. oil in a wok or pan
- Stir-fry onion and ginger for a few seconds
- Add broccoli, beef and the remaining ingredients
- Stir-fry 30 seconds over high heat

Serving
Serve with rice 3

Did you know?
- The name broccoli (derived from the Latin word *Brachium*, meaning arm or branch) was given by the ancient Romans, because the vegetable resembles a miniature tree. Broccoli contains calcium, phosphorus, potassium, and vitamins A and C.
- The color of green vegetables can be preserved when they are boiled for a brief period and transferred immediately to cold water.

Spiced Coconut Beef
Rendang

Ingredients

1½ lbs. beef (beef chuck can be used)
½ cup coconut milk (shake can)
3½ cups water
1 piece (¼ inch) fresh ginger
3 lime leaves (or 3 square inches lemon peel)
3 cloves garlic
3 candlenuts
1 shallot
1 tbs. dark brown sugar
½ tbs. paprika powder

1 tsp. crushed dried red chili or ground red chilies *(sambal)*, adjust amount to taste
½ tsp. ground lemongrass
½ tsp. ground coriander
¼ tsp. ground turmeric
½ tsp. ground galangal
¼ tsp. ground pepper
¼ tsp. ground cumin
½ tsp. shrimp paste
1 tsp. lime juice
2 tsp. salt

Preparation

• Cut beef into 2½x1x1 inch pieces
• Bring 2 cups of water in a pot to a boil
• Add beef; cook 5 minutes
• Set aside beef; discard broth
• Peel and slice ginger
• Peel shallots and garlic
• Grind shallots, garlic and candlenuts until smooth (add 3 tbs. water to facilitate grinding)
• Mix all ingredients with the remaining water in a pot; bring to a boil
• Cover pot; simmer 45 minutes until meat is tender and liquid becomes thick, stirring occasionally to prevent burning

Serving

Serve with rice for 3

Tips

• The lime juice not only adds flavor, but also tenderizes the meat during cooking.
• The dish can be prepared in large quantities and frozen until needed.

Did you know?

Rendang originated in Sumatra. However, it has been integrated into many other regions and has become an indispensable traditional dish in Java. In Sumatra buffalo meat is used for *Rendang*, but in Java it is substituted with beef.

Pork

Pork on Skewers in Red Sauce
Sweet and Sour Pork
Fried Pork Chops in Soy Sauce
Fried Ribs
Barbecue Ribs
Fried Sausage with Five-Spices
Stewed Pork in Soy Sauce
Sauerkraut with Sausage

Pork on Skewers in Red Sauce
Sate Bumbu Rujak

Ingredients
Seasoning sauce

½ cup coconut milk (shake can)
1 piece (¼ inch) fresh ginger
2 tbs. ground red chilies *(sambal)*, adjust amount to taste
1 tbs. dark brown sugar
1 tbs. fried shallots
½ tsp. ground coriander
½ tsp. shrimp paste
1 tsp. fried garlic
½ tsp. salt

1½ lbs. pork
20 bamboo skewers
1 tbs. vegetable oil

Meat
Preparation
- Cut meat into cubes of 1×¾×½ inch; peel and slice ginger
- Mix all ingredients for the seasoning sauce in a small pot
- Cook 3 minutes or until thick, stirring occasionally to prevent burning
- Set aside 8 tbs. sauce; use the remainder to marinate the meat for 1 hour or overnight. Thread 5 pieces of meat onto each skewer. The meat should be arranged on the skewer so that the cubes run lengthwise.

Cooking meat on charcoal grill (for the best result)
- Grill meat 4-5 minutes each side until meat is cooked

Cooking meat in oven (alternative)
- Preheat oven to the highest setting
- Put meat on a double layer of aluminum foil brushed with oil
- In a gas oven place meat on the floor of oven (not on rack). In an electric oven place meat on a rack closest to the heat source. Keep the skewers away from the heat to prevent burning. Leave oven door ajar to allow skewers to project outward. Cook 5-6 minutes each side until meat is cooked.

Serving
- Heat the reserve sauce; mix with the meat before serving
- Makes 20 skewers. Serve with rice

Sweet and Sour Pork
Kolobak

Ingredients

Sauce

1   piece (½ inch) fresh ginger
¾   cup water
1   small can chunky pineapple
2   tbs. frozen green peas
1½ tbs. cornstarch
2   tbs. ketchup
½   tsp. ground red chilies *(sambal)*, adjust
      amount to taste
½   tsp. fried garlic
1½ tsp. vinegar
2½ tsp. sugar
½   tsp. salt

Meat

1½ cups vegetable oil
1   lb. pork
1   tbs. cooking wine
3   tbs. cornstarch
1   tbs. soy sauce

Preparation

Sauce

- Peel and slice ginger
- Mix cornstarch with 2 tbs. water
- Mix sugar with 3 tbs. water in a small pot
- Heat sugar solution until light brown, stirring occasionally to prevent burning
- Add ginger and the remaining water
- Bring to a short boil
- Stir in cornstarch and the remaining ingredients; simmer 1 minute

Meat

- Slice pork thinly
- Marinate pork with a mixture of wine and soy sauce 15 minutes
- Coat meat pieces with cornstarch
- Heat oil in a wok or frying pan
- Deep-fry meat 2 minutes

Serving

- Pour sauce over warm fried meat
- Serve warm with rice for 2

Did you know? Chilies are rich in Vitamins A and C. The levels of both vitamins increase with the degree of ripeness. Consequently, red chilies have a significantly higher vitamin content than the green ones.

Fried Pork Chops in Soy Sauce
Daging Babi Goreng Saus Kecap

Ingredients

Meat

2   pieces pork chops (1 lb.)
2   cloves garlic
1   tbs. cooking wine
1   tbs. cornstarch
1   tbs. soy sauce
1   tsp. sugar
½   cup vegetable oil

Sauce

1   piece (½ inch) fresh ginger
1   clove garlic
1   scallion
1   tbs. white vinegar
1   tbs. vegetable oil
3   tbs. soy sauce
1   tsp. sugar

Preparation

Meat

• Peel and crush garlic
• Mix garlic, wine, sugar and soy sauce
• Marinate meat with mixture 1 hour
• Heat oil in a wok or frying pan
• Coat meat with cornstarch; fry 4 minutes each side or until meat is cooked

Sauce

• Peel and chop garlic an ginger
• Wash and chop scallion
• Heat oil in a small pot
• Stir-fry ginger and garlic 1 minute
• Add all other ingredients
• Bring sauce to a short boil

Serving

• Pour hot sauce on warm meat, then sprinkle chopped scallion
• Serve with rice for 2

Fried Ribs
Tulang Iga Goreng

Ingredients
1½ lbs. pork ribs (use ribs with thick meat)
1   egg white
1   tbs. cooking wine
2   tbs. soy sauce
2   tbs. cornstarch
1   tsp. ground turmeric
¼   tsp. ground pepper
1   tsp. garlic powder
2   tsp. sugar
½   tsp. salt
1   cup vegetable oil

Preparation
• Chop pork ribs into serving size
• Prepare marinade by mixing all ingredients, except oil and ribs
• Marinate rib pieces 1 hour or overnight in the refrigerator
• Heat oil in a wok or frying pan
• Deep-fry rib pieces 1 minute each side

Serving
Serve with rice for 3

Barbecue Ribs
Tulang Iga Panggang

Ingredients
1   lb. pork ribs
2   cloves garlic
2   tbs. soy sauce
1   tbs. sugar
1   tbs. honey
½   tsp. five-spice powder

Preparation
• Peel and mince garlic
• Prepare marinade by mixing all ingredients, except honey and ribs
• Marinate ribs 1 hour or overnight in the refrigerator
• Preheat oven to the highest setting
• Put ribs on a double layer of aluminum foil brushed with oil
• In a gas oven place ribs on the floor of oven (not on rack). In an electric oven place ribs on a rack closest to the heat source.
• Cook 8 minutes each side until meat is cooked
• Baste with honey while ribs are still hot

Serving
• Serve with rice for 2

Tip to store garlic
Peeled garlic will remain fresh for a long time when soaked in vegetable oil and kept refrigerated. This method eliminates the need to peel fresh garlic for every recipe. The oil, in which the nice garlic aroma develops, can be used for cooking. Prepare peeled garlic this way in your spare moments, and you will find it a pleasure not to have to peel garlic each time you cook.

Fried Sausage with Five-Spices
Sosis Rempah

Ingredients
½   lb. ground pork
½   lb. shrimp
1   scallion
1   egg
1   cup cornstarch
2   tbs. fish sauce
1   tbs. soy sauce
1   tsp. five-spice powder
½   tsp. ground pepper
2   tsp. garlic powder
1   cup vegetable oil

Preparation
• Wash, peel and grind shrimp
• Wash and chop scallion
• Break egg, remove shell
• Mix all ingredients, except cornstarch and oil
• Roll mixture to form sausages
• Coat sausages with cornstarch
• Heat oil in a wok or frying pan
• Deep-fry sausage until cooked and crispy

Serving
• Cut sausages into slices; serve with rice

Tip to peel garlic easily
Keep garlic skin dry. Press the flat side of a knife gently on a garlic clove to loosen the skin. Now the skin can be easily removed from the clove by hand.

Stewed Pork in Soy Sauce
Babi Kecap

Ingredients
1½ lbs. pork (pork shoulder can be used)
¼ cup soy sauce
½ cup water
2 tbs. sugar
½ tsp. five-spice powder
2 tsp. fried garlic

Preparation
• Cut pork into big pieces
• Broil pork 10-15 minutes each side; set aside
• Mix all ingredients (except pork) in a pot
• Bring mixture to a boil
• Add meat; cover pot
• Simmer 30 minutes until pork is tender, turning meat occasionally

Serving
Serve with rice for 3

Did you know how soy sauce is made?
The process consists of five steps:
• Preparation of mold broth: A mixture of cooked soy beans and roasted, crushed wheat are mixed and inoculated with a pure starter mold culture of *Aspergillus oryzae*. The mixture is spread onto wooden trays and incubated at room temperature for 2-3 days.
• Treatment of raw materials: Soy beans are soaked in running water for 10-15 hours at room temperature and cooked under 10-12 psi pressure for about 1 hour. Wheat is prepared by roasting and crushing.
• Mash fermentation and aging: The mold broth is added to a mixture of treated soy beans and wheat. The mixture is put onto porous bamboo trays and incubated at room temperature for 2 days. Then brine containing 17-22% salt is added and the mash is allowed to ferment for 3-4 months.
• Pressing and refining: The liquid is separated from the mash using a hydraulic press.
• Pasteurization: The liquid is pasteurized at 70-80° C.

Sauerkraut with Sausage
Tumis Kubis Asam

Ingredients

¼ lb. smoked sausages	2 tbs. vegetable oil
1 lb. sauerkraut	2 tbs. sour cream
2 stalks cilantro	3 tbs. soy sauce
2 cloves garlic	2 tbs. sugar
1 onion	2 cups water

Preparation

• Drain sauerkraut
• Soak sauerkraut in water for 30 seconds; drain and remove water thoroughly by pressing sauerkraut with spatula against the strainer
• Cut sausages into thin slices
• Peel and slice garlic and onion
• Wash and chop cilantro
• Heat oil in a wok or frying pan
• Stir-fry garlic 1 minute
• Add onion and sausage pieces; stir-fry 2-3 minutes
• Add sauerkraut, soy sauce, sugar and sour cream; stir-fry 5 minutes
• Add and mix chopped cilantro shortly before serving

Serving
Serve with rice for 3

Memories
This recipe is my own creation, inspired by a refrigerator containing only sauerkraut and sausage. This recipe is related to Western recipes that usually use a combination of sauerkraut and sausage, but the use of soy sauce and cilantro gives my recipe its Oriental character. Cilantro (or coriander leaf), with its roots still attached, is available in well-stocked supermarkets. It can be kept fresh for at least a week by soaking the root in water and covering the leafy part with a plastic bag.

Sauerkraut is made by mixing shredded cabbage with salt, then allowing lactic acid fermentation to occur. In the fermentation process, the sugars of the cabbage are converted primarily to lactic and acetic acids, ethyl alcohol, and carbon dioxide. Sauerkraut is sold in sealed plastic bags that are kept under refrigeration, but can also be bought in cans and glass containers.

Lamb/Goat

Sautéed Lamb/Goat with Tomato
Lamb/Goat Curry

Sautéed Lamb/Goat with Tomato
Daging Kambing Masak Tomat

Ingredients

¾ lb. goat (can be replaced with lamb)
5   thin strips orange peel
1   piece (¼ inch) fresh ginger
1   medium ripe tomato
1   small bell pepper
1   small onion
1   scallion
2   tbs. vegetable oil
½   tbs. cornstarch
2   tbs. soy sauce
3   tbs. water
½   tsp. sugar
½   tsp. salt

Preparation

• Cut meat into thin slices
• Peel and chop ginger
• Wash and chop scallion
• Cut onion, tomato and bell pepper into big pieces; separate onion layers
• Mix cornstarch with 1 tbs. water
• Heat oil in a wok or nonstick pan
• Add ginger, orange peel strips and bell pepper; stir-fry 1 minute
• Add meat; stir-fry 2 minutes
• Add onion, scallion and tomato; stir-fry 1 minute
• Add salt, sugar, soy sauce and cornstarch solution; stir-fry 1 minute

Serving

Serve with rice for 2

Did you know?

Goat meat is much more popular in Asia than in America. One of the most popular types of meat is from the domesticated goat (*Capra Aegragus*) castrated before he reaches puberty. In many parts of Asia this is the favorite for curries and falls under the generic term of mutton.

Lamb/Goat Curry
Gulai Kambing

Ingredients
1½ lbs. goat (can be replaced with lamb)
½   cup coconut milk (shake can before use)
2½ cups water
1   stick cinnamon bark
2   pods star anise
1   piece (1 inch) fresh ginger
3   lime leaves (or 3 square inches lemon peel)
2   tbs. fried shallots
½   tbs. fried garlic
1   tsp. ground red chilies *(sambal)*, adjust amount to taste
½   tsp. ground lemongrass
½   tsp. ground coriander
1   tsp. ground galangal
1   tsp. ground turmeric
¼   tsp. ground pepper
¼   tsp. ground cumin
¼   tsp. ground clove
2   tsp. salt

Preparation
- Cut meat into 2-inch cubes
- Peel and slice ginger
- Mix water and all ingredients (except meat) in a pot
- Bring broth to a boil
- Add meat to the boiling water piece by piece so that broth continues boiling
- Cover pot; simmer 45 minutes or until meat is tender

Serving
- Sprinkle with fried shallots before serving
- Serve with rice for 4

Did you know?
Gulai was originally introduced to Indonesia by the Hindus from India. It has been modified to suit the Indonesian taste and has been adopted into the traditional Indonesian cuisine.

Desserts & Beverages

Double Layer Pudding
Coconut Pudding
Sweet Yucca Snack
Sweet Rice with Coconut Dip
Sweet Coconut Rice Balls
Custard Pastries
Cat Tongue Cookies
Double Layer Cake
Sweet and Spicy Fruit Salad
Pear with Honey
Fruit Cocktail
Avocado-Cocktail & Avocado Drink

Double Layer Pudding
Agar Dua Lapis

Ingredients

White layer
1 package agar-agar powder (7 g)
1 small can fruit cocktail
3 egg whites
1 cup water
4 tbs. sugar

Sauce
2 cups milk
2 egg yolks
3 tbs. cornstarch
3 tbs. sugar
1½ tbs. rum
½ tsp. vanilla extract

Chocolate layer
1 package agar-agar powder (7 g)
2¾ cups milk
2 tbs. cocoa powder
5 tbs. sugar

Preparation

White layer
- Drain fruit liquid in a pot; add water, sugar and agar-agar
- Boil 5 minutes while stirring until dissolved; turn heat off
- Beat egg whites until stiff (3 minutes)
- Add fruit and egg whites to agar-agar mixture; mix well
- Pour into a mold; let it set

Sauce
- Mix egg yolks with 3 tbs. milk; beat lightly with a fork
- Mix cornstarch with 3 tbs. milk
- Heat the remaining milk in a pot
- Stir in sugar, cornstarch and egg yolk
- Bring to a short boil; turn heat off
- Add vanilla extract and rum
- Let it cool

Chocolate layer
- Disperse cocoa powder in milk
- Add sugar and agar-agar
- Cook 7 minutes while stirring until dissolved; let it cool for 8 minutes
- Pour on top of white layer; let it set

Serving
- Flip pudding on a flat plate
- Decorate with strawberries
- Serve pudding slices with sauce
- Serves 8

Coconut Pudding
Agar Degan

Ingredients
1   package agar-agar powder (7 g)
½   lb. young coconut slivers (available frozen in Asian markets)
¼   lb. dark brown sugar
1   cup coconut milk (shake can)
2   cups water
2   eggs

Preparation
• Mix agar-agar, coconut milk, water and brown sugar in a small pot
• Cook 6 minutes while stirring until dissolved
• Beat eggs lightly with a fork
• Add egg slowly to mixture while stirring
• Add coconut slivers to mixture
• Bring to a short boil
• Pour into cups to set

Serving
Serve cool or at room temperature as a snack or dessert

Did you know?
• Agar-agar solution starts to gel at 86º F (30º C). The gel is heat resistant and melts only when heated at above 185º F (85º C). It is a nonnutritive carbohydrate, therefore it does not yield food energy.

Sweet Yucca Snack
Getuk Lindri

Ingredients
½   lbs. yucca root
½   cup freshly grated coconut
2   cups water
2   tbs. dark brown sugar
½   tsp. salt

Preparation
- Peel the outer brown bark and the inside pink layer of yucca
- Cut yucca into ½ inch thick pieces
- Add salt to water in a pot; bring to a boil
- Add yucca; cover pot; simmer 15 minutes
- Discard water; add sugar to yucca; mash yucca while warm
- Shape yucca dough into round disks of 1½ inches diameter and ¼ inch thick
- Coat yucca pieces with grated coconut

Serving
- Serve at room temperature as a snack or dessert
- Makes 20 pieces

Tip
If fresh coconut is unavailable, use dried coconut flakes, which are available in cans or plastic bags.

Did you know?
- Yucca is the edible root of the yucca or cassava plant. The root is 6-36 inches long and 1.5-6 inches wide. It is cylindrical, conical or oval, with a pink or cream-colored peel that is covered by a thin brown bark. Yucca root is the fourth most important source of calories in the human diet in tropical regions of the world and is consumed in a wide variety of forms. Yucca root is rich in carbohydrate (mostly starch), but low in proteins and most other nutrients. Yucca originated in the Americas and was taken by the Spanish and Portuguese traders to Africa, India and Southeast Asia in the sixteenth and seventeenth centuries. In Indonesia, yucca root is fermented using an innoculum of *Amylomyces* and *Endomycopsis* to produce a moist delicious product called *tape*.

Sweet Rice with Coconut Dip
Ketan Srikaya

Ingredients

Rice
¼ lb. sweet rice
1 cup water
2 tbs. coconut milk (shake can)
¼ tsp. salt

Dip
1 egg
¼ cup coconut milk (shake can)
1½ cups water
5 tbs. dark brown sugar
½ tsp. salt

Preparation

Rice
- Soak sweet rice in water for 1 hour
- Drain rice; steam 20 minutes
- Add coconut milk and salt; mix well
- Place cooked rice on a flat container
- Spread ½ inch thick layer of rice on a sheet of aluminum foil
- Cut rice bed into big square pieces

Dip
- Beat egg lightly with a fork in a bowl
- Add sugar, coconut milk and water
- Pour mixture into heatproof cups; steam 10 minutes

Serving
- Serve rice with coconut dip

Sweet Coconut Rice Balls
Klepon

Ingredients
1   lb. sweet rice flour
1   cup freshly grated coconut
¼   cup dark brown sugar
1   cup lukewarm water
8   cups water
1   tbs. vegetable oil
¾   tsp. salt
1   drop of juice concentrate of *pandan* leaves (or food coloring)

Preparation
- Mix flour, lukewarm water, oil, salt and *pandan* to form a firm but flexible dough; use immediately to prevent drying
- Take about 1 heaping tsp. dough; roll into a ball about ¾ inch in diameter
- Press the center of the balls with a finger to make a well
- Fill each well with ¼-½ tsp. sugar; pinch the edges of the well to enclose the sugar completely (Sugar should not be visible from outside). If the balls are not completely sealed, sugar will leak out upon boiling.
- Roll the balls gently with the palms of the hands to shape
- Boil filled balls (about 10 balls at a time) 3 minutes or until balls float to the surface. The sugar melts upon boiling but should remain inside.
- Remove balls with a slotted spoon and roll them (while still warm) in grated coconut so the surface of the balls is completely coated

Serving
- Serve as a snack or dessert
- Makes 30 balls

Tips
- Use fresh grated coconut for the best taste. If fresh coconut is unavailable, use dried coconut flakes, which are available in cans or plastic bags.
- The original Indonesian *klepon* is green from the juice of green *pandan* (screwpine) leaves. This juice is added not only for the color, but also for its delightful yet subtle aroma and flavor. If it is unavailable, food coloring may be used. Although the characteristic gentle aroma of the *pandan* leaves is missing, the recipe will still deliver wonderful *klepon*. Everyone who has tasted *klepon* will always remember the sensation of biting into this soft rice ball with the melted brown sugar inside.

Custard Pastries
Kue Sus

Ingredients

Pastry

¼ lb. all-purpose flour
¼ lb. margarine
1½ cups water
6 eggs
¼ tsp. salt

Filling

2 cups milk
4 egg yolks
4 tbs. cornstarch
5 tbs. sugar
2 tbs. rum
1 tsp. vanilla extract
¼ tsp. salt

Preparation

Pastry

- Place water, margarine and salt in a pot; bring to a short boil
- Turn heat off; add flour; mix until smooth
- Simmer 10 minutes, then let it cool
- Add and mix eggs one by one
- Put dough in forcing bag; squirt spiral shape pieces onto cookie sheet
- Bake 15-20 minutes at 425º F

Filling

- Mix milk, salt and cornstarch
- Beat egg yolks with sugar until white
- Stir in milk mixture
- Cook over medium heat while stirring until thick
- Let it cool; add rum and mix

Serving

- Cut pastries across and fill
- Makes 20-25 pastries

Cat Tongue Cookies
Lidah Kucing

Ingredients
3 egg whites
¼ lb. all-purpose flour
¼ lb. margarine
¼ lb. sugar

Preparation
• Beat egg whites for 1 minute or until stiff; set aside
• Beat margarine and sugar for 5 minutes or until mixture turns white
• Add flour; mix
• Add egg whites; mix
• Place mixture into a forcing bag; squirt the dough onto cookie sheet
• Bake 15 minutes at 300°F

Serving
Makes 50-100 (depending on size) cat tongue cookies

Tip
Make this recipe when you have left over egg whites (for example after baking the double-layer cake).

Did you know?
• Cat tongue cookies are so named because of their shape.
• Egg white contains 88% water and 11% protein. The proteins are highly digestible and because they contain all the essential amino acids required to maintain life and promote growth and health. When an egg white is beaten, air bubbles are trapped in the proteins, creating foam. The foam becomes a carrier of air for leavening and contributes to the lightness of certain foods.

Double Layer Cake
Kue Spiku

Ingredients

Yellow layer

4 egg whites
10 egg yolks
1¼ cups powdered sugar
6 oz. margarine
2 oz. butter
3 tbs. all-purpose flour
3 tbs. cornstarch
1 tsp. vanilla

Chocolate layer

4 egg whites
10 egg yolks
1¼ cups powdered sugar
6 oz. margarine
2 oz. butter
2½ tbs. all-purpose flour
2½ tbs. cornstarch
1 tbs. cocoa powder

Icing

1 oz. butter
1 tbs. sweetened condensed milk

Preparation

Yellow layer

- Melt margarine and butter; set aside
- Mix flour and cornstarch
- Beat egg yolks, sugar and vanilla until white and thick
- Beat egg whites until white and stiff
- Mix flour mixture with egg yolk mixture
- Add egg whites; mix gently
- Add melted margarine butter mixture; mix gently
- Pour mixture onto a nonstick tray (12x9½ inches)
- Bake 40 minutes at 325° F

Chocolate layer

- Prepare like the yellow layer, except mix cocoa powder with flour and cornstarch, and omit vanilla extract

Icing

- Melt butter; add condensed milk

Layer Assembling

- Place one layer on a flat surface
- Spread on icing
- Place the other layer on top of it
- Cut ¼ inch from all sides; discard
- Cut cake into 2 long pieces, then slice

Serving

- Serve cool or at room temperature

Tips

- Cake can be stored refrigerated for one week.
- To prevent sticking of the cake to the tray, smear the tray with margarine, then coat the margarine with a thin layer of flour.

Sweet and Spicy Fruit Salad
Rujak Manis

Ingredients

Sauce
5	tbs. dark brown sugar
1	tbs. soy sauce
3	tbs. lime juice
3	tbs. water
1½	tsp. ground red chilies (*sambal*), adjust amount to taste

Fruits & Vegetables
½	firm Granny Smith apple
1	kirby cucumber
½	fresh pineapple
½	unripe mango
¼	small yam
1	starfruit
¼	jicama

Preparation
• Peel pineapple, mango, cucumber and yam
• Cut all fruits and vegetables into serving pieces
• Mix all fruit and vegetable pieces
• Prepare sauce by mixing all ingredients in a small bowl

Serving
• Pour sauce over fruit and vegetables shortly before serving
• Serve cold or at room temperature as an appetizer, dessert or snack for 4

Tips
• Any combination of fruits and vegetables can be used.
• The browning in apple pieces, which is due to an enzymatic oxidation, can be prevented by soaking the cut pieces briefly in a diluted solution of limes, lemons, vitamin C or citric acid.

Did you know?
Jicama originated in Mexico. The vegetable tastes similar to an apple, but has a texture like a water chestnut. It contains high 88% water and 1.4% protein. It is available in well-stocked supermarkets and in Asian and Mexican groceries. The skin of jicama is tough and should be peeled completely with a knife.

Pear with Honey
Buah Per dan Madu

Ingredients
2   pears
1   lemon
1   tbs. margarine or butter
½   tbs. cornstarch
4   tbs. honey
2   tbs. water
2   tbs. rum

Preparation
- Mix cornstarch with water; set aside
- Squeeze lemon
- Mix lemon juice, honey and rum
- Peal and cut pears into ½ inch slices
- Marinate pears overnight in juice mixture
- Remove pears and heat marinade
- Add cornstarch solution while stirring; set aside
- Melt butter in a pan
- Fry pears 5-10 minutes over medium heat until brown and soft

Serving
- Pour hot juice over hot pears
- Serves 2

Fruit Cocktail
Es Campur

Ingredients
5   pieces canned lichees
1   tbs. frozen young coconut slivers (available frozen in Asian markets)
1   tbs. gelatin snack pieces (prepared according to package description)
3   tbs. water or liquid from canned fruit
2   tbs. canned chunky pineapple
1   tbs. canned jackfruit pieces
2   tbs. shaved or crushed ice
1   tbs. fruity syrup
1   tsp. condensed milk

Preparation
• Prepare gelatin snack as described in the package. Cut gelatin snack into small square
  pieces
• Cut jack fruit into small pieces
• Mix water, gelatin pieces, young coconut slivers and all fruit pieces in a glass
• On top add shaved ice, then condensed milk and syrup

Serving
• Serve as snack, appetizer, or dessert

Avocado-Fruit Cocktail & Avocado Coffee Drink
Es Teler & Es Apokat

Ingredients

Es Teler
¼   avocado
2   tbs. frozen young coconut slivers
     (available frozen in asian markets)
3   tbs. coconut milk (shake can)
2   tbs. shaved or crushed ice
2   tbs. jack fruit pieces
2   tbs. fruity syrup
3   tbs. water

Es Apokat
¼   avocado
1   cup milk
2   tbs. sugar
2   tsp. instant coffee

Preparation

Es Teler
- Using a spoon scoop out avocado meat into serving pieces
- Cut jack fruit into small pieces
- Add to a glass in the following order: syrup, jack fruit, coconut slivers, avocado, water and coconut milk
- Add shaved ice on top

Es Apokat
- Mix milk, sugar and instant coffee in a glass
- Using a spoon scoop out avocado meat into serving pieces and place in a glass
- Pour milk mixture onto avocado pieces

Serving
Serve as a snack, appetizer or dessert

Tips
- *Es apokat* can be served hot or cool. Add ice to serve cool or heat milk to serve hot.
- Instant coffee can be replaced with cocoa powder.

Did you know?
In Mexican Foods, avocado is used for dips, salads, and soups. In Indonesia, avocado is used in drinks. It is always best to use a ripe avocado. Avocado is ripe when it yields to gentle pressure. Keep avocado at room temperature for a few days to ripen it. To obtain the meat, halve avocado lengthwise, remove the pit and scoop out the meat with a spoon. Avocado contains potassium and vitamin C.

GLOSSARY (*Indonesian*-English)

Acar ketimun: pickled cucumber
Agar-agar: agar
Apokat: avocado
Arak ketan: alcoholic drink made from fermented glutinous rice
Asam: tamarind, sour
Ayam: chicken
Asparagus: asparagus

Babi: pig; pork
Bawang Bombay: onion
Bawang goreng: fried onion
Bawang merah: shallot
Bawang putih: garlic
Bebek (Javanese): duck
Bihun: rice noodles
Brokoli: broccoli
Bumbu: spices, ingredients
Buncis: string beans
Bungkus: wrapped
Buntut: oxtail

Cabai: chili
Cabai besar: large chili
Cabai rawit: small hot chili
Camilan: snack
Campur: mixed, to mix
Cengkeh: cloves
Cobek: stone mortar and pestle for grinding spices
Cumi-cumi: calamari

Daging: meat, usually means beef unless otherwise specified
Dalang: puppeteer
Dan: and
Daun: leaf
Daun bawang: scallion
Daun jeruk: lime leaf
Degan: young coconut meat

Es: ice
Es teler: name of drink (fruit cocktail)
Gado-gado: name of food (salad with peanut dressing)
Gamelan: Indonesian xylophonic orchestra
Goreng: fried, to fry
Gula: sugar
Gula Jawa: "Java sugar" or brown sugar from the aren palm tree
Gulai: curry dish

Hati: liver

Ikan: fish
Isi: stuffed
Jagung: corn

Jahe: ginger
Jamu: Indonesian herbal drink
Jeruk: orange; tangerine
Jeruk limau: lime
Jintan: cumin seed

Kacang: peanut
Kambing: goat
Kangkung: a kind of water spinach
Kayu manis: cinnamon
Kecambah: bean sprouts
Kecap asin: soy sauce
Kecap ikan: fish sauce
Kecap manis: sweet soy sauce
Kelapa: coconut
Kembang: flower
Kembang kol: cauliflower
Kemiri: candlenut
Kencur: zedoary or cutchery
Kentang: potato
Kepiting: crab
Kerang: clam
Kerang kepah: scallop
Kerbau: water buffalo
Ketan: glutinous, sweet, or sticky rice
Ketumbar: coriander seed
Klepon: name of food (snack made from glutinous rice flour)
Kolobak: name of food (sweet sour pork)
Kroket: name of food (fried meat rolls)
Krupuk: Indonesian cracker
Kuah: soup
Kuali: wok
Kubis: cabbage
Kue: cake

Kukus: steamed, to steam
Kunir (kunyit): turmeric
Labu Siam: chayote
Laos (langkuas): galangal
Lapis: layer
Lemper: name of food (glutinous rice stuffed with spiced chicken)
Lodeh: vegetable coconut soup
Lumpia: name of food (spingrolls)

Manis: sweet
Martabak: name of food (turnover stuffed with meat)
Masak: cook
Mi: noodles
Minyak: oil
Minyak sesam: sesame oil

Nasi: cooked rice
Nasi goreng: fried rice

Pala: nutmeg
Panggang: barbecue
Pangsit: wonton
Paprika: bell pepper
Pastel: pie
Pecel: name of food (vegetable with peanut dressing)
Pedas: hot; spicy
Perkedel: patty
Pindang: cooked
Puding: pudding
Pisang: banana

Rebung: bamboo shoot
Rempah: spices; seasonings
Rendang: name of food (spiced coconut beef)
Rijsttafel: Dutch word refers to Indonesian meal comprises of rice and a variety of side dishes
Rissoles: name of food (crispy fried ragout pocket)
Rujak: spicy food

Sambal: chili sauce
Santan: coconut sauce
Sate: grilled meat on skewers
Saus: sauce
Saus tiram: oyster sauce
Sawah: rice terrace
Sayur: vegetable
Selada: lettuce
Selada air: watercress
Selamatan: Javanese communal feast

Semur: stew
Sereh: lemongrass
Siomai: name of food (filled pockets of noodle dough)
Sosis: sausage
Soto: curry soup
Spiku: layered cake
Stupa: Buddhist shrine
Sup: soup

Tahu: beancurd or tofu
Tauge: bean sprouts
Telur: egg
Tempe: fermented soy beans
Terasi: shrimp paste
Terung: eggplant
Tiram: oyster
Tomat: tomato
Toko: store
Tuak: fermented sap of the inflorescence of coconut palm
Tulang: bone
Tulang iga: backbone; sparerib
Tumis: sauté
Tutup: closed

Udang: shrimp
Ulekan: see *cobek*

Wajan (Javanese)*:* wok
Wayang kulit: shadow puppet
Wonton: name of food (filled pockets of noodle dough)

Index

Sweet Rice Filled with Chicken *(Lemper)* **30**
Tomato Chicken Soup with Vegetables *(Sup Merah)* **45**

Clams
Sautéed Clams in Soy Sauce *(Sambal Goreng Kerang)* **75**

Crab
Egg Fu-Yong *(Telur Fu-yong)* **73**
Asparagus Soup with Crab Meat *(Kuah Asparagus)* **44**

Desserts/Sweets
Avocado-Fruit Cocktail & Avocado Drink *(Es Teler & Es Apokat)* **131**
Cat Tongue Cookies *(Lidah Kucing)* **126**
Coconut Pudding *(Agar Degan)* **121**
Custard Pastries *(Kue Sus)* **125**
Double Layer Cake *(Kue Spiku)* **127**
Double Layer Pudding *(Agar Dua Lapis)* **120**
Fried Plantain *(Pisang Goreng)* **31**
Fruit Cocktail *(Es Campur)* **130**
Pear with Honey *(Buah Per dan Madu)* **129**
Sweet and Spicy Fruit Salad *(Rujak Manis)* **128**
Sweet Coconut Rice Balls *(Klepon)* **124**
Sweet Rice with Coconut Dip *(Ketan Srikaya)* **123**
Sweet Yucca Snack *(Getuk Lindri)* **122**

Duck
Crispy Duck *(Bebek Goreng)* **99**
Duck with Lime Sauce *(Bebek Panggang Saus Jeruk Limau)* **98**

Fish
Fried Fish Cutlets in Curry Sauce *(Ikan Pindang Tumis)* **68**
Fried Fish in Red Coconut Sauce *(Ikan Bumbu Rujak)* **69**
Fried Fish in Soy Sauce *(Ikan Goreng Saus Kecap)* **70**
Fried Fish in Sweet and Sour Sauce *(Ikan Goreng Asam Manis)* **67**
Fried Fish Rolls in Sweet and Sour Sauce *(Ikan Bungkus Asam Manis)* **71**

Lamb
Lamb/Goat Curry *(Gulai Kambing)* **118**
Lamb Turnover *(Martabak)* **33**
Sautéed Lamb/Goat with Tomato *(Daging Kambing Masak Tomat)* **117**

Noodles
Chicken Noodle Soup *(Kuah Mi Ayam)* **46**
Crispy Noodles *(Ifu Mi)* **65**
Crispy Rice Noodles *(Bihun Goreng)* **63**
Curry Rice Noodles *(Bihun Kunir)* **62**
Fried Noodles *(Mi Goreng)* **64**

Oxtail
Oxtail Tomato Soup *(Tomat Sup Buntut)* **48**
Oxtail Vegetable Soup *(Sup Buntut)* **49**

Pickle
Pickled Cucumber *(Acar Ketimun)* **51**

Pork
Barbecue Ribs *(Tulang Iga Panggang)* **112**
Fried Pork Chops in Soy Sauce *(Daging Babi Goreng Saus Kecap)* **110**
Fried Ribs *(Tulang Iga Goreng)* **111**
Fried Sausage with Five-Spices *(Sosis Rempah)* **113**
Pork on Skewers in Red Sauce *(Sate Bumbu Rujak)* **108**
Stewed Pork in Soy Sauce *(Babi Kecap)* **114**
Stuffed Chinese Eggplant *(Terung Isi)* **54**
Sweet and Sour Pork *(Kolobak)* **109**

Prawns/Shrimp
Chicken Liver with Shrimp and Coconut *(Sambal Goreng Hati)* **94**
Fried Prawns with Tomato Sauce *(Udang Goreng Saus Tomat)* **77**
Fried Rice with Shrimp *(Nasi Goreng Udang)* **60**
Fried Shrimp and Calamari with Five-Spices *(Udang dan Cumi-cumi Goreng Rempah)* **74**
Sautéed Prawn *(Udang Tumis)* **80**
Shrimp Snacks *(Camilan Udang)* **37**
Stir-Fried Shrimp with Ginger *(Udang Tumis Jahe)* **72**
Stir-Fried Shrimp with Tomato and Bell Pepper *(Udang Tumis Tomat dan Paprika)* **78**
Sweet and Sour Shrimp with Fried Potatoes *(Selada Udang)* **79**

Rice
Fried Rice with Bacon *(Nasi Goreng Bacon)* **58**
Ginger Fried Rice *(Nasi Goreng Jahe)* **59**
Fried Rice with Shrimp *(Nasi Goreng Udang)* **60**
Fried Rice with Spicy Sausage *(Nasi Goreng Sosis)* **61**

Salad
Chicken Salad *(Ayam Selada)* **97**
Salad with Peanut Dressing *(Gado-gado)* **55**
Sweet and Spicy Fruit Salad *(Rujak Manis)* **128**

Sate
Beef on Skewers *(Sate Komo)* **101**
Chicken on Skewers with Peanut Dressing *(Sate Ayam)* **84**
Pork on Skewers in Red Sauce *(Sate Bumbu Rujak)* **108**

Sauce
Lime Sauce for Baked Duck *(Saus Jeruk Limau)* **98**
Peanut Dressing for Salad *(Bumbu Gado-gado)* **55**
Peanut Sauce for Chicken on Skewers *(Bumbu Sate Ayam)* **84**
Sauce for Egg Fu-Yong *(Saus Telur Fu-Yong)* **73**
Sauce for Fried Chicken *(Saus Ayam Goreng)* **85**
Sauce for Fried Fish *(Bumbu Ikan Goreng)* **69**
Sauce for Fried Pork Chop *(Bumbu Babi Goreng)* **110**
Sauce for Fried Springroll *(Saus Lumpia)* **32**
Sauce for Sweet and Spicy Fruit Salad *(Rujak Manis)* **128**
Seasoning Sauce for Barbecue Chicken *(Bumbu Ayam Panggang)* **88**
Seasoning Sauce for Barbecue Spareribs *(Bumbu Tulang Iga Panggang)* **112**
Seasoning Sauce for Fried Chicken *(Bumbu Ayam Goreng)* **95**
Seasoning Sauce for Fried Ribs *(Bumbu Tulang Iga Goreng)* **111**
Seasoning Sauce for Pork on Skewers *(Sate Bumbu Rujak)* **108**
Sweet and Sour Sauce for Fried Fish *(Saus Asam Manis)* **67**

Scallops
Scallops in Oyster Sauce *(Kerang Kepah Saus Tiram)* **82**
Spicy Scallops *(Kerang Kepah Pedas)* **76**

Shrimp (see prawns)

Snacks (see appetizers)

Soups
Asparagus Soup with Crab Meat *(Kuah Asparagus)* **44**
Chayote Soup *(Kuah Waluh)* **43**
Chicken Noodle Soup *(Kuah Mi Ayam)* **46**
Curry Chicken Soup *(Soto Ayam)* **47**
Oxtail Tomato Soup *(Tomat Sup Buntut)* **48**
Oxtail Vegetable Soup *(Sup Buntut)* **49**
Stir-Fried Chicken in Broth *(Ayam Bakmoi)* **90**
Tomato Chicken Soup with Vegetables *(Sup Merah)* **45**
Vegetable Coconut Soup *(Sayur Lodeh)* **41**
Vegetable Soup with Filled Omelet *(Kuah Sayur dan Telur Goreng Isi)* **42**

Vegetables
Bamboo Shoots in Coconut Sauce *(Sambal Goreng Rebung)* **53**
Fried Cauliflower *(Kembang Kol Goreng)* **56**
Fried Corn Patties *(Perkedel Jagung)* **51**
Salad with Peanut Dressing *(Gado-gado)* **55**
Sautéed Vegetables with Beancurd *(Sambal Goreng Tahu)* **52**
Stuffed Chinese Eggplant *(Terung Isi)* **54**

U.S. and Metric Conversion Table

	U.S.	**Metric**
Volume:	1 cup	240 milliliters
Weight:	1 ounce (oz.)	28.35 grams
	1 pound (lb.)	0.45 kilograms
Length:	1 inch	2.54 centimeters
Temperature:	250°F	121°C
	300°F	149°C
	350°F	177°C
	400°F	204°C
	450°F	232°C
	500°F	260°C

Notes

Notes

Notes

Taste of Indonesia: Recipes from the Spice Islands
Is available on CD ROM for both Mac and PC
Full color photographs of all recipes plus lots more stuff
Contact publisher for information

SLG BOOKS
PO Box 9465 Berkeley, CA 94709
Tel: (510) 525-1134
Fax: (510) 525-2632
Email Indonesia@slgbooks.com
URL: www.slgbooks.com